Food and Agriculture Organization of the United Nations

International Fisheries
Instruments with Index

Agreement for the Implementation of the Provisions
of the United Nations Convention on the Law of the Sea
of 10 December 1982 relating to the Conservation and Management
of Straddling Fish Stocks and Highly Migratory Fish Stocks

Agreement to Promote Compliance with International
Conservation and Management Measures
by Fishing Vessels on the High Seas

Code of Conduct for Responsible Fisheries

Division for Ocean Affairs and the Law of the Sea
Office of Legal Affairs
United Nations • New York, 1998

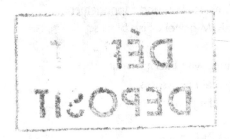

UNITED NATIONS PUBLICATION

Sales No. E.98.V.11

ISBN 92-1-133603-1

Preface

This publication, prepared jointly by the Division for Ocean Affairs and the Law of the Sea, Office of Legal Affairs, of the United Nations and the Food and Agriculture Organization of the United Nations (FAO), contains the official texts of three important international fisheries instruments adopted in recent years under United Nations or FAO auspices. These texts are supplemented by introductory remarks providing the background information relating to the process of their negotiation and adoption, as well as by an integrated subject index.

CONTENTS

I. Agreement for the Implementation of the Provisions of the United
Nations Convention on the Law of the Sea of 10 December 1982
relating to the Conservation and Management of Straddling Fish
Stocks and Highly Migratory Fish Stocks

II. Agreement to Promote Compliance with International Conservation and Management Measures by Fishing Vessels on the High Seas

Page

III. Code of Conduct for Responsible Fisheries

Page

I. Agreement for the Implementation of the Provisions of the United Nations Convention on the Law of the Sea of 10 December 1982 relating to the Conservation and Management of Straddling Fish Stocks and Highly Migratory Fish Stocks

Background

1.	The United Nations Conference on Straddling Fish Stocks and Highly Migratory Fish Stocks was convened pursuant to paragraph 1 of General Assembly resolution 47/192 of 22 December 1992 in accordance with the mandate agreed upon at the United Nations Conference on Environment and Development.

2.	The United Nations Conference on Environment and Development, held at Rio de Janeiro from 3 to 14 June 1992, adopted Agenda 21, paragraph 17.49 of which reads as follows:

> "States should take effective action, including bilateral and multilateral cooperation, where appropriate at the subregional, regional and global levels, to ensure that high seas fisheries are managed in accordance with the provisions of the United Nations Convention on the Law of the Sea. In particular, they should:

> "...

> "(e)	Convene, as soon as possible, an intergovernmental conference under United Nations auspices, taking into account relevant activities at the subregional, regional and global levels, with a view to promoting effective implementation of the provisions of the United Nations Convention on the Law of the Sea on straddling fish stocks and highly migratory fish stocks. The conference, drawing, inter alia, on scientific and technical studies by the Food and Agriculture Organization of the United Nations (FAO), should identify and assess existing problems related to the conservation and management of such fish stocks, and consider means of improving cooperation on fisheries among States, and formulate appropriate recommendations. The work and the results of the conference should be fully consistent with the provisions of the United Nations Convention on the Law of the Sea, in particular the rights and obligations of coastal States and States fishing on the high seas." [1]

3.	The General Assembly, in its resolution 47/192, recalled Agenda 21, in particular chapter 17, programme area C, relating to the sustainable use and conservation of marine living resources of the high seas, and decided that the Conference, in accordance with the mandate quoted above, should take into account relevant activities at the subregional,

---

[1] Report of the United Nations Conference on Environment and Development, Rio de Janeiro, 3-14 June 1992 (United Nations publication, Sales No. E.93.I.8 and corrigenda), vol. I: Resolutions adopted by the Conference, resolution 1, annex II, para. 17.49.

regional and global levels, with a view to promoting effective implementation of the provisions of the United Nations Convention on the Law of the Sea on straddling fish stocks and highly migratory fish stocks. The Assembly further decided that the Conference, drawing, inter alia, on scientific and technical studies by FAO, should: (a) identify and assess existing problems related to the conservation and management of such fish stocks; (b) consider means of improving fisheries cooperation among States; and (c) formulate appropriate recommendations.

4.   The General Assembly also reaffirmed that the work and results of the Conference should be fully consistent with the provisions of the United Nations Convention on the Law of the Sea, in particular the rights and obligations of coastal States and States fishing on the high seas, and that States should give full effect to the high seas fisheries provisions of the Convention with regard to fisheries populations whose ranges lay both within and beyond exclusive economic zones (straddling fish stocks) and highly migratory fish stocks.

5.   By the same resolution, the General Assembly invited relevant specialized agencies, particularly FAO, and other appropriate organs, organizations and programmes of the United Nations system, as well as regional and subregional fisheries organizations, to contribute relevant scientific and technical studies and reports. It also invited relevant non-governmental organizations from developed and developing countries to contribute to the Conference within the areas of their competence and expertise.

6.   Pursuant to General Assembly resolutions 47/192, 48/194 of 21 December 1993 and 49/121 of 19 December 1994, the following sessions of the United Nations Conference on Straddling Fish Stocks and Highly Migratory Fish Stocks were held at United Nations Headquarters in New York:[2]

- First session: 19 to 23 April 1993;
- Second session: 12 to 30 July 1993;
- Third session: 14 to 31 March 1994;
- Fourth session: 15 to 26 August 1994;
- Fifth session: 27 March to 12 April 1995;
- Sixth session: 24 July to 4 August 1995.

7.   The representatives of the following States participated in the sessions of the Conference: Albania, Algeria, Angola, Antigua and Barbuda, Argentina, Australia, Austria, Bahamas, Bahrain, Bangladesh, Barbados, Belarus, Belgium, Belize, Benin, Brazil, Bulgaria, Burundi, Cameroon, Canada, Cape Verde, Chile, China, Colombia, Congo, Cook Islands, Costa Rica, Côte d'Ivoire, Cuba, Cyprus, Democratic People's Republic of Korea, Denmark, Djibouti, Ecuador, Egypt, El Salvador, Eritrea, Estonia, Fiji, Finland, France, Gabon, Gambia, Germany, Ghana, Greece, Grenada, Guatemala, Guinea, Guinea-Bissau, Guyana, Honduras, Hungary, Iceland, India, Indonesia, Iran (Islamic Republic of), Ireland,

---

[2] Reports on each of the sessions are contained in A/CONF.164/9 (first (organizational) session), A/CONF.164/16 and Corr.1 (second session), A/CONF.164/20 (third session), A/CONF.164/25 (fourth session), A/CONF.164/29 (fifth session) and A/CONF/164/36 (sixth session).

Israel, Italy, Jamaica, Japan, Kazakhstan, Kenya, Kiribati, Latvia, Lebanon, Lesotho, Libyan Arab Jamahiriya, Liechtenstein, Lithuania, Luxembourg, Madagascar, Malaysia, Maldives, Mali, Malta, Marshall Islands, Mauritania, Mauritius, Mexico, Micronesia (Federated States of), Morocco, Myanmar, Namibia, Netherlands, New Zealand, Nicaragua, Niger, Nigeria, Niue, Norway, Pakistan, Palau, Panama, Papua New Guinea, Peru, Philippines, Poland, Portugal, Qatar, Republic of Korea, Romania, Russian Federation, Saint Lucia, Samoa, Saudi Arabia, Senegal, Seychelles, Sierra Leone, Singapore, Solomon Islands, South Africa, Spain, Sri Lanka, Suriname, Sweden, Switzerland, Syrian Arab Republic, Thailand, Togo, Tonga, Trinidad and Tobago, Tunisia, Turkey, Tuvalu, Uganda, Ukraine, United Arab Emirates, United Kingdom of Great Britain and Northern Ireland, United Republic of Tanzania, United States of America, Uruguay, Vanuatu, Venezuela, Viet Nam, Zambia and Zimbabwe. The representative of the European Community participated in the sessions without the right to vote.

The following associate members of a regional commission were represented as observers at the sessions: Montserrat and United States Virgin Islands.

The following national liberation movement was represented as observer at the first session: Pan Africanist Congress of Azania.

The following specialized agencies were represented as observers at the sessions: Food and Agriculture Organization of the United Nations (FAO), United Nations Educational, Scientific and Cultural Organization (UNESCO) and World Bank.

The Intergovernmental Oceanographic Commission (IOC) of UNESCO, the United Nations Development Programme (UNDP) and the United Nations Environment Programme (UNEP) were also present as observers at the sessions.

The following intergovernmental organizations were represented as observers at the sessions: Asian-African Legal Consultative Committee, Commission on the Indian Ocean, Inter-American Tropical Tuna Commission, International Commission for the Conservation of Atlantic Tunas, International Council for the Exploration of the Sea, International Maritime Satellite Organization, International Whaling Commission, Latin American Organization for the Development of Fisheries, Ministerial Conference on Fisheries Cooperation among African States bordering the Atlantic Ocean, North Atlantic Salmon Conservation Organization, Northwest Atlantic Fisheries Organization, Organization of African Unity, Organisation for Economic Cooperation and Development, South Pacific Commission, South Pacific Permanent Commission and South Pacific Forum Fisheries Agency.

The following non-governmental organizations were represented as observers at the sessions: Alaska Marine Conservation Council, Alaska Public Interest Research Group, American Oceans Campaign, American Society of International Law, Association Algérienne pour la Protection de la Nature et de l'Environnement, Association Tunisienne pour la Protection de la Nature et de l'Environnement, Association of the Bar of the City of New York, Atlantic Salmon Federation, Bering Sea Fisherman's Association, Both Ends, Canadian Oceans Caucus, Center for Development of International Law, Center for Marine Conservation, Centre de

Recherches pour le Développement des Technologies Intermédiares de Pêche, Comité Catholique Contre la Faim et pour le Développement, Confederación de Trabajadores Portuarios, Gente de Mar y Pesqueros de Chile, Confederación Nacional de Pescadores Artesanales de Chile, Coordinadora de Tripulantes Pesqueros Industriales del Cono Sur de América Latina, Council on Ocean Law, Earth Council, Earth Island Institute, Earthtrust, Environmental Defense Fund, Federación Nacional de Cooperativas Pesqueras del Ecuador, Federation of Japan Tuna Fisheries Cooperative Associations, Fish, Food and Allied Workers, Fisheries Council of Canada, Four Directions Council, Friends of the Earth International, Friends World Committee for Consultations (Quaker United Nations Office), Fundación Hernandiana, Global Education Associates, Greenpeace International, Groupement d'Intérêt Économique, International Coalition of Fisheries Associations, International Coastal and Ocean Organization, International Collective in Support of Fishworkers, International Confederation of Free Trade Unions, International Institute for Sustainable Development, International Law Association, International Ocean Institute, International Union for the Conservation of Nature and Natural Resources (IUCN), Japan Fisheries Association, Kandune Self-Help Water Project, Marine Environmental Research Institute, Namibian Food and Allied Workers Union, National Audubon Society, National Wildlife Federation, Nationwide Coalition of Fisherfolks for Aquatic Reform, Natural Resources Defense Council, Netherlands National Committee for IUCN, Newfoundland and Labrador Environmental Association, Newfoundland Inshore Fisheries Association, Oceans Institute of Canada, Ocean Trust, Overseas Fishery Cooperation Foundation, Pamalakaya (National United Movement of Fisherfolk - Philippines), Red Mexicana de Acción frente al Libre Comercio, Réserve Internationale Maritime en Mediterranée Occidentale, Samoan Association of Non-governmental Organizations, Sindicato de Obreros Marítimos Unidos, SONAR (Save Our Northwest Atlantic Resources), Trickle Up Program, United Nations Association in Canada, United Nations Association-United Kingdom, United Nations Environment and Development-United Kingdom Committee, Wildlife Conservation Society, Women and Fisheries Network, World Wide Fund for Nature, World Wide Fund Suisse.

8.　　　At its first meeting, the Conference elected Mr. Satya N. Nandan (Fiji) as its Chairman. The Conference also elected as Vice-Chairmen the representatives of the following States: Chile, Italy and Mauritania.

9.　　　The Conference adopted its agenda (A/CONF.164/5) and rules of procedure (A/CONF.164/6) at its first session.

10.　　At the second session, the Conference devoted the first three days to general debate, following which the Chairman outlined the key issues on which there was general agreement. At the same session, the Conference proceeded to examine the issues relating to straddling fish stocks and highly migratory fish stocks as contained in the document entitled "A guide to the issues before the Conference prepared by the Chairman" (A/CONF.164/10). At the end of the second session, the Chairman prepared a negotiating text (A/CONF.164/13), which the Conference considered at the third session.

11.　　Also at the third session, the Conference established two open-ended working groups to consider the information papers, prepared by FAO at the request of the Conference, on the precautionary approach to fisheries management and on management reference points. Mr. Andrés Couve (Chile) and Mr. Andrew Rosenberg (United States of America) served as chairmen of the working groups. The results of the work of the two working groups are contained in documents A/CONF.164/WP.1 and WP.2. At the end of the third session, the Chairman submitted a revision of his negotiating text (A/CONF.164/13/Rev.1), which reflected the work of the working groups.

12.   At the fourth session, the Chairman prepared a new revision of his negotiating text in the form of a binding instrument, entitled "Draft Agreement for the Implementation of the Provisions of the United Nations Convention on the Law of the Sea of 10 December 1982 relating to the Conservation and Management of Straddling Fish Stocks and Highly Migratory Fish Stocks" (A/CONF.164/22). At the end of the fifth session, the Chairman prepared a revised text of the Draft Agreement (A/CONF.164/22/Rev.1).

13.   At the sixth session, the Conference considered the revised text of the Draft Agreement (A/CONF.164/22/Rev.1), as well as suggested drafting changes and editorial improvements (A/CONF.164/CRP.7). Following the deliberations of the Conference, the Chairman proposed for adoption a "Draft Agreement for the Implementation of the Provisions of the United Nations Convention on the Law of the Sea of 10 December 1982 relating to the Conservation and Management of Straddling Fish Stocks and Highly Migratory Fish Stocks" (A/CONF.164/33).

14.   On 4 August 1995, the Conference adopted without a vote the Agreement for the Implementation of the Provisions of the United Nations Convention on the Law of the Sea of 10 December 1982 relating to the Conservation and Management of Straddling Fish Stocks and Highly Migratory Fish Stocks, as well as resolution I on early and effective implementation of the Agreement and resolution II concerning reports on developments by the Secretary-General of the United Nations. The two resolutions are annexed to the Final Act of the Conference (A/CONF.164/38). In doing so, the Conference discharged the mandate given to it by the General Assembly in its resolution 47/192.

15.   The Conference decided to resume its sixth session on 4 December 1995 for a ceremony of signature of the Agreement and the Final Act. The Conference requested the Secretariat to prepare the final text of the Agreement, incorporating necessary editing and drafting changes and ensuring concordance among the six language versions (A/CONF.164/37). Pursuant to its article 37, the Agreement was opened for signature from 4 December 1995 to 4 December 1996.

Agreement for the Implementation of the Provisions of the United Nations Convention on the Law of the Sea of 10 December 1982 relating to the Conservation and Management of Straddling Fish Stocks and Highly Migratory Fish Stocks

The States Parties to this Agreement,

Recalling the relevant provisions of the United Nations Convention on the Law of the Sea of 10 December 1982,

Determined to ensure the long-term conservation and sustainable use of straddling fish stocks and highly migratory fish stocks,

Resolved to improve cooperation between States to that end,

Calling for more effective enforcement by flag States, port States and coastal States of the conservation and management measures adopted for such stocks,

Seeking to address in particular the problems identified in chapter 17, programme area C, of Agenda 21 adopted by the United Nations Conference on Environment and Development, namely, that the management of high seas fisheries is inadequate in many areas and that some resources are overutilized; noting that there are problems of unregulated fishing, over-capitalization, excessive fleet size, vessel reflagging to escape controls, insufficiently selective gear, unreliable databases and lack of sufficient cooperation between States,

Committing themselves to responsible fisheries,

Conscious of the need to avoid adverse impacts on the marine environment, preserve biodiversity, maintain the integrity of marine ecosystems and minimize the risk of long-term or irreversible effects of fishing operations,

Recognizing the need for specific assistance, including financial, scientific and technological assistance, in order that developing States can participate effectively in the conservation, management and sustainable use of straddling fish stocks and highly migratory fish stocks,

Convinced that an agreement for the implementation of the relevant provisions of the Convention would best serve these purposes and contribute to the maintenance of international peace and security,

Affirming that matters not regulated by the Convention or by this Agreement continue to be governed by the rules and principles of general international law,

Have agreed as follows:

PART I

GENERAL PROVISIONS

Article 1
Use of terms and scope

1.   For the purposes of this Agreement:
        (a)   "Convention" means the United Nations Convention on the
Law of the Sea of 10 December 1982;
        (b)   "conservation and management measures" means measures
to conserve and manage one or more species of living marine resources that
are adopted and applied consistent with the relevant rules of international law
as reflected in the Convention and this Agreement;
        (c)   "fish" includes molluscs and crustaceans except those
belonging to sedentary species as defined in article 77 of the Convention; and
        (d)   "arrangement" means a cooperative mechanism established
in accordance with the Convention and this Agreement by two or more States
for the purpose, *inter alia*, of establishing conservation and management
measures in a subregion or region for one or more straddling fish stocks or
highly migratory fish stocks.
2.   (a)   "States Parties" means States which have consented to be
bound by this Agreement and for which the Agreement is in force.
        (b)   This Agreement applies, *mutatis mutandis*:
        (i)   to any entity referred to in article 305, paragraph 1 (c), (d)
                 and (e), of the Convention and
        (ii)   subject to article 47, to any entity referred to as an
                 "international organization" in Annex IX, article 1, of the
                 Convention
which becomes a Party to this Agreement, and to that extent "States Parties"
refers to those entities.
3.   This Agreement applies *mutatis mutandis* to other fishing entities
whose vessels fish on the high seas.

Article 2
Objective

The objective of this Agreement is to ensure the long-term
conservation and sustainable use of straddling fish stocks and highly
migratory fish stocks through effective implementation of the relevant
provisions of the Convention.

Article 3
Application

1.   Unless otherwise provided, this Agreement applies to the
conservation and management of straddling fish stocks and highly migratory
fish stocks beyond areas under national jurisdiction, except that articles 6 and
7 apply also to the conservation and management of such stocks within areas
under national jurisdiction, subject to the different legal regimes that apply
within areas under national jurisdiction and in areas beyond national
jurisdiction as provided for in the Convention.
2.   In the exercise of its sovereign rights for the purpose of exploring
and exploiting, conserving and managing straddling fish stocks and highly
migratory fish stocks within areas under national jurisdiction, the coastal
State shall apply *mutatis mutandis* the general principles enumerated in
article 5.

3.   States shall give due consideration to the respective capacities of developing States to apply articles 5, 6 and 7 within areas under national jurisdiction and their need for assistance as provided for in this Agreement. To this end, Part VII applies *mutatis mutandis* in respect of areas under national jurisdiction.

Article 4
Relationship between this Agreement and the Convention

Nothing in this Agreement shall prejudice the rights, jurisdiction and duties of States under the Convention. This Agreement shall be interpreted and applied in the context of and in a manner consistent with the Convention.

PART II

CONSERVATION AND MANAGEMENT OF STRADDLING FISH STOCKS AND HIGHLY MIGRATORY FISH STOCKS

Article 5
General principles

In order to conserve and manage straddling fish stocks and highly migratory fish stocks, coastal States and States fishing on the high seas shall, in giving effect to their duty to cooperate in accordance with the Convention:

(a)   adopt measures to ensure long-term sustainability of straddling fish stocks and highly migratory fish stocks and promote the objective of their optimum utilization;

(b)   ensure that such measures are based on the best scientific evidence available and are designed to maintain or restore stocks at levels capable of producing maximum sustainable yield, as qualified by relevant environmental and economic factors, including the special requirements of developing States, and taking into account fishing patterns, the interdependence of stocks and any generally recommended international minimum standards, whether subregional, regional or global;

(c)   apply the precautionary approach in accordance with article 6;

(d)   assess the impacts of fishing, other human activities and environmental factors on target stocks and species belonging to the same ecosystem or associated with or dependent upon the target stocks;

(e)   adopt, where necessary, conservation and management measures for species belonging to the same ecosystem or associated with or dependent upon the target stocks, with a view to maintaining or restoring populations of such species above levels at which their reproduction may become seriously threatened;

(f)   minimize pollution, waste, discards, catch by lost or abandoned gear, catch of non-target species, both fish and non-fish species, (hereinafter referred to as non-target species) and impacts on associated or dependent species, in particular endangered species, through measures including, to the extent practicable, the development and use of selective, environmentally safe and cost-effective fishing gear and techniques;

(g)   protect biodiversity in the marine environment;

(h)   take measures to prevent or eliminate overfishing and excess fishing capacity and to ensure that levels of fishing effort do not exceed those commensurate with the sustainable use of fishery resources;

(i)   take into account the interests of artisanal and subsistence fishers;

(j)   collect and share, in a timely manner, complete and accurate data concerning fishing activities on, *inter alia,* vessel position, catch of target and non-target species and fishing effort, as set out in Annex I, as well as information from national and international research programmes;

(k)   promote and conduct scientific research and develop appropriate technologies in support of fishery conservation and management; and

(l)   implement and enforce conservation and management measures through effective monitoring, control and surveillance.

Article 6
Application of the precautionary approach

1.   States shall apply the precautionary approach widely to conservation, management and exploitation of straddling fish stocks and highly migratory fish stocks in order to protect the living marine resources and preserve the marine environment.

2.   States shall be more cautious when information is uncertain, unreliable or inadequate. The absence of adequate scientific information shall not be used as a reason for postponing or failing to take conservation and management measures.

3.   In implementing the precautionary approach, States shall:

(a)   improve decision-making for fishery resource conservation and management by obtaining and sharing the best scientific information available and implementing improved techniques for dealing with risk and uncertainty;

(b)   apply the guidelines set out in Annex II and determine, on the basis of the best scientific information available, stock-specific reference points and the action to be taken if they are exceeded;

(c)   take into account, *inter alia,* uncertainties relating to the size and productivity of the stocks, reference points, stock condition in relation to such reference points, levels and distribution of fishing mortality and the impact of fishing activities on non-target and associated or dependent species, as well as existing and predicted oceanic, environmental and socio-economic conditions; and

(d)   develop data collection and research programmes to assess the impact of fishing on non-target and associated or dependent species and their environment, and adopt plans which are necessary to ensure the conservation of such species and to protect habitats of special concern.

4.   States shall take measures to ensure that, when reference points are approached, they will not be exceeded. In the event that they are exceeded, States shall, without delay, take the action determined under paragraph 3 (b) to restore the stocks.

5.   Where the status of target stocks or non-target or associated or dependent species is of concern, States shall subject such stocks and species to enhanced monitoring in order to review their status and the efficacy of conservation and management measures. They shall revise those measures regularly in the light of new information.

6.   For new or exploratory fisheries, States shall adopt as soon as possible cautious conservation and management measures, including, *inter alia*, catch limits and effort limits. Such measures shall remain in force until there are sufficient data to allow assessment of the impact of the fisheries on the long-term sustainability of the stocks, whereupon conservation and management measures based on that assessment shall be implemented. The

latter measures shall, if appropriate, allow for the gradual development of the fisheries.

7.   If a natural phenomenon has a significant adverse impact on the status of straddling fish stocks or highly migratory fish stocks, States shall adopt conservation and management measures on an emergency basis to ensure that fishing activity does not exacerbate such adverse impact. States shall also adopt such measures on an emergency basis where fishing activity presents a serious threat to the sustainability of such stocks. Measures taken on an emergency basis shall be temporary and shall be based on the best scientific evidence available.

Article 7
Compatibility of conservation and management measures

1.   Without prejudice to the sovereign rights of coastal States for the purpose of exploring and exploiting, conserving and managing the living marine resources within areas under national jurisdiction as provided for in the Convention, and the right of all States for their nationals to engage in fishing on the high seas in accordance with the Convention:

(a)   with respect to straddling fish stocks, the relevant coastal States and the States whose nationals fish for such stocks in the adjacent high seas area shall seek, either directly or through the appropriate mechanisms for cooperation provided for in Part III, to agree upon the measures necessary for the conservation of these stocks in the adjacent high seas area;

(b)   with respect to highly migratory fish stocks, the relevant coastal States and other States whose nationals fish for such stocks in the region shall cooperate, either directly or through the appropriate mechanisms for cooperation provided for in Part III, with a view to ensuring conservation and promoting the objective of optimum utilization of such stocks throughout the region, both within and beyond the areas under national jurisdiction.

2.   Conservation and management measures established for the high seas and those adopted for areas under national jurisdiction shall be compatible in order to ensure conservation and management of the straddling fish stocks and highly migratory fish stocks in their entirety. To this end, coastal States and States fishing on the high seas have a duty to cooperate for the purpose of achieving compatible measures in respect of such stocks. In determining compatible conservation and management measures, States shall:

(a)   take into account the conservation and management measures adopted and applied in accordance with article 61 of the Convention in respect of the same stocks by coastal States within areas under national jurisdiction and ensure that measures established in respect of such stocks for the high seas do not undermine the effectiveness of such measures;

(b)   take into account previously agreed measures established and applied for the high seas in accordance with the Convention in respect of the same stocks by relevant coastal States and States fishing on the high seas;

(c)   take into account previously agreed measures established and applied in accordance with the Convention in respect of the same stocks by a subregional or regional fisheries management organization or arrangement;

(d)   take into account the biological unity and other biological characteristics of the stocks and the relationships between the distribution of the stocks, the fisheries and the geographical particularities of the region concerned, including the extent to which the stocks occur and are fished in areas under national jurisdiction;

(e)   take into account the respective dependence of the coastal States and the States fishing on the high seas on the stocks concerned; and
(f)   ensure that such measures do not result in harmful impact on the living marine resources as a whole.

3.   In giving effect to their duty to cooperate, States shall make every effort to agree on compatible conservation and management measures within a reasonable period of time.

4.   If no agreement can be reached within a reasonable period of time, any of the States concerned may invoke the procedures for the settlement of disputes provided for in Part VIII.

5.   Pending agreement on compatible conservation and management measures, the States concerned, in a spirit of understanding and cooperation, shall make every effort to enter into provisional arrangements of a practical nature. In the event that they are unable to agree on such arrangements, any of the States concerned may, for the purpose of obtaining provisional measures, submit the dispute to a court or tribunal in accordance with the procedures for the settlement of disputes provided for in Part VIII.

6.   Provisional arrangements or measures entered into or prescribed pursuant to paragraph 5 shall take into account the provisions of this Part, shall have due regard to the rights and obligations of all States concerned, shall not jeopardize or hamper the reaching of final agreement on compatible conservation and management measures and shall be without prejudice to the final outcome of any dispute settlement procedure.

7.   Coastal States shall regularly inform States fishing on the high seas in the subregion or region, either directly or through appropriate subregional or regional fisheries management organizations or arrangements, or through other appropriate means, of the measures they have adopted for straddling fish stocks and highly migratory fish stocks within areas under their national jurisdiction.

8.   States fishing on the high seas shall regularly inform other interested States, either directly or through appropriate subregional or regional fisheries management organizations or arrangements, or through other appropriate means, of the measures they have adopted for regulating the activities of vessels flying their flag which fish for such stocks on the high seas.

PART III

**MECHANISMS FOR INTERNATIONAL COOPERATION
CONCERNING STRADDLING FISH STOCKS AND HIGHLY
MIGRATORY FISH STOCKS**

Article 8
Cooperation for conservation and management

1.   Coastal States and States fishing on the high seas shall, in accordance with the Convention, pursue cooperation in relation to straddling fish stocks and highly migratory fish stocks either directly or through appropriate subregional or regional fisheries management organizations or arrangements, taking into account the specific characteristics of the subregion or region, to ensure effective conservation and management of such stocks.

2.   States shall enter into consultations in good faith and without delay, particularly where there is evidence that the straddling fish stocks and highly migratory fish stocks concerned may be under threat of over-exploitation or where a new fishery is being developed for such stocks. To this end, consultations may be initiated at the request of any interested State with a view to establishing appropriate arrangements to ensure conservation and management of the stocks. Pending agreement on such arrangements, States shall observe the provisions of this Agreement and shall act in good faith and with due regard to the rights, interests and duties of other States.

3.   Where a subregional or regional fisheries management organization or arrangement has the competence to establish conservation and management measures for particular straddling fish stocks or highly migratory fish stocks, States fishing for the stocks on the high seas and relevant coastal States shall give effect to their duty to cooperate by becoming members of such organization or participants in such arrangement, or by agreeing to apply the conservation and management measures established by such organization or arrangement. States having a real interest in the fisheries concerned may become members of such organization or participants in such arrangement. The terms of participation in such organization or arrangement shall not preclude such States from membership or participation; nor shall they be applied in a manner which discriminates against any State or group of States having a real interest in the fisheries concerned.

4.   Only those States which are members of such an organization or participants in such an arrangement, or which agree to apply the conservation and management measures established by such organization or arrangement, shall have access to the fishery resources to which those measures apply.

5.   Where there is no subregional or regional fisheries management organization or arrangement to establish conservation and management measures for a particular straddling fish stock or highly migratory fish stock, relevant coastal States and States fishing on the high seas for such stock in the subregion or region shall cooperate to establish such an organization or enter into other appropriate arrangements to ensure conservation and management of such stock and shall participate in the work of the organization or arrangement.

6.   Any State intending to propose that action be taken by an intergovernmental organization having competence with respect to living resources should, where such action would have a significant effect on conservation and management measures already established by a competent subregional or regional fisheries management organization or arrangement,

consult through that organization or arrangement with its members or participants. To the extent practicable, such consultation should take place prior to the submission of the proposal to the intergovernmental organization.

Article 9
Subregional and regional fisheries management organizations and arrangements

1.   In establishing subregional or regional fisheries management organizations or in entering into subregional or regional fisheries management arrangements for straddling fish stocks and highly migratory fish stocks, States shall agree, *inter alia*, on:

(a)   the stocks to which conservation and management measures apply, taking into account the biological characteristics of the stocks concerned and the nature of the fisheries involved;

(b)   the area of application, taking into account article 7, paragraph 1, and the characteristics of the subregion or region, including socio-economic, geographical and environmental factors;

(c)   the relationship between the work of the new organization or arrangement and the role, objectives and operations of any relevant existing fisheries management organizations or arrangements; and

(d)   the mechanisms by which the organization or arrangement will obtain scientific advice and review the status of the stocks, including, where appropriate, the establishment of a scientific advisory body.

2.   States cooperating in the formation of a subregional or regional fisheries management organization or arrangement shall inform other States which they are aware have a real interest in the work of the proposed organization or arrangement of such cooperation.

Article 10
Functions of subregional and regional fisheries management organizations and arrangements

In fulfilling their obligation to cooperate through subregional or regional fisheries management organizations or arrangements, States shall:

(a)   agree on and comply with conservation and management measures to ensure the long-term sustainability of straddling fish stocks and highly migratory fish stocks;

(b)   agree, as appropriate, on participatory rights such as allocations of allowable catch or levels of fishing effort;

(c)   adopt and apply any generally recommended international minimum standards for the responsible conduct of fishing operations;

(d)   obtain and evaluate scientific advice, review the status of the stocks and assess the impact of fishing on non-target and associated or dependent species;

(e)   agree on standards for collection, reporting, verification and exchange of data on fisheries for the stocks;

(f)   compile and disseminate accurate and complete statistical data, as described in Annex I, to ensure that the best scientific evidence is available, while maintaining confidentiality where appropriate;

(g)   promote and conduct scientific assessments of the stocks and relevant research and disseminate the results thereof;

(h)   establish appropriate cooperative mechanisms for effective monitoring, control, surveillance and enforcement;

(i)   agree on means by which the fishing interests of new members of the organization or new participants in the arrangement will be accommodated;

(j)   agree on decision-making procedures which facilitate the adoption of conservation and management measures in a timely and effective manner;

(k)   promote the peaceful settlement of disputes in accordance with Part VIII;

(l)   ensure the full cooperation of their relevant national agencies and industries in implementing the recommendations and decisions of the organization or arrangement; and

(m)   give due publicity to the conservation and management measures established by the organization or arrangement.

Article 11
New members or participants

In determining the nature and extent of participatory rights for new members of a subregional or regional fisheries management organization, or for new participants in a subregional or regional fisheries management arrangement, States shall take into account, *inter alia*:

(a)   the status of the straddling fish stocks and highly migratory fish stocks and the existing level of fishing effort in the fishery;

(b)   the respective interests, fishing patterns and fishing practices of new and existing members or participants;

(c)   the respective contributions of new and existing members or participants to conservation and management of the stocks, to the collection and provision of accurate data and to the conduct of scientific research on the stocks;

(d)   the needs of coastal fishing communities which are dependent mainly on fishing for the stocks;

(e)   the needs of coastal States whose economies are overwhelmingly dependent on the exploitation of living marine resources; and

(f)   the interests of developing States from the subregion or region in whose areas of national jurisdiction the stocks also occur.

Article 12
Transparency in activities of subregional and regional fisheries management organizations and arrangements

1.   States shall provide for transparency in the decision-making process and other activities of subregional and regional fisheries management organizations and arrangements.

2.   Representatives from other intergovernmental organizations and representatives from non-governmental organizations concerned with straddling fish stocks and highly migratory fish stocks shall be afforded the opportunity to take part in meetings of subregional and regional fisheries management organizations and arrangements as observers or otherwise, as appropriate, in accordance with the procedures of the organization or arrangement concerned. Such procedures shall not be unduly restrictive in this respect. Such intergovernmental organizations and non-governmental organizations shall have timely access to the records and reports of such organizations and arrangements, subject to the procedural rules on access to them.

Article 13
Strengthening of existing organizations and arrangements

States shall cooperate to strengthen existing subregional and regional fisheries management organizations and arrangements in order to improve their effectiveness in establishing and implementing conservation and management measures for straddling fish stocks and highly migratory fish stocks.

Article 14
Collection and provision of information and cooperation in scientific research

1.   States shall ensure that fishing vessels flying their flag provide such information as may be necessary in order to fulfil their obligations under this Agreement. To this end, States shall in accordance with Annex I:

(a)   collect and exchange scientific, technical and statistical data with respect to fisheries for straddling fish stocks and highly migratory fish stocks;

(b)   ensure that data are collected in sufficient detail to facilitate effective stock assessment and are provided in a timely manner to fulfil the requirements of subregional or regional fisheries management organizations or arrangements; and

(c)   take appropriate measures to verify the accuracy of such data.

2.   States shall cooperate, either directly or through subregional or regional fisheries management organizations or arrangements:

(a)   to agree on the specification of data and the format in which they are to be provided to such organizations or arrangements, taking into account the nature of the stocks and the fisheries for those stocks; and

(b)   to develop and share analytical techniques and stock assessment methodologies to improve measures for the conservation and management of straddling fish stocks and highly migratory fish stocks.

3.   Consistent with Part XIII of the Convention, States shall cooperate, either directly or through competent international organizations, to strengthen scientific research capacity in the field of fisheries and promote scientific research related to the conservation and management of straddling fish stocks and highly migratory fish stocks for the benefit of all. To this end, a State or the competent international organization conducting such research beyond areas under national jurisdiction shall actively promote the publication and dissemination to any interested States of the results of that research and information relating to its objectives and methods and, to the extent practicable, shall facilitate the participation of scientists from those States in such research.

Article 15
Enclosed and semi-enclosed seas

In implementing this Agreement in an enclosed or semi-enclosed sea, States shall take into account the natural characteristics of that sea and shall also act in a manner consistent with Part IX of the Convention and other relevant provisions thereof.

Article 16
Areas of high seas surrounded entirely by an area under
the national jurisdiction of a single State

1.   States fishing for straddling fish stocks and highly migratory fish stocks in an area of the high seas surrounded entirely by an area under the national jurisdiction of a single State and the latter State shall cooperate to establish conservation and management measures in respect of those stocks in the high seas area. Having regard to the natural characteristics of the area, States shall pay special attention to the establishment of compatible conservation and management measures for such stocks pursuant to article 7. Measures taken in respect of the high seas shall take into account the rights, duties and interests of the coastal State under the Convention, shall be based on the best scientific evidence available and shall also take into account any conservation and management measures adopted and applied in respect of the same stocks in accordance with article 61 of the Convention by the coastal State in the area under national jurisdiction.   States shall also agree on measures for monitoring, control, surveillance and enforcement to ensure compliance with the conservation and management measures in respect of the high seas.
2.   Pursuant to article 8, States shall act in good faith and make every effort to agree without delay on conservation and management measures to be applied in the carrying out of fishing operations in the area referred to in paragraph 1. If, within a reasonable period of time, the fishing States concerned and the coastal State are unable to agree on such measures, they shall, having regard to paragraph 1, apply article 7, paragraphs 4, 5 and 6, relating to provisional arrangements or measures. Pending the establishment of such provisional arrangements or measures, the States concerned shall take measures in respect of vessels flying their flag in order that they not engage in fisheries which could undermine the stocks concerned.

PART IV

NON-MEMBERS AND NON-PARTICIPANTS

Article 17
Non-members of organizations and non-participants
in arrangements

1.   A State which is not a member of a subregional or regional fisheries management organization or is not a participant in a subregional or regional fisheries management arrangement, and which does not otherwise agree to apply the conservation and management measures established by such organization or arrangement, is not discharged from the obligation to cooperate, in accordance with the Convention and this Agreement, in the conservation and management of the relevant straddling fish stocks and highly migratory fish stocks.
2.   Such State shall not authorize vessels flying its flag to engage in fishing operations for the straddling fish stocks or highly migratory fish stocks which are subject to the conservation and management measures established by such organization or arrangement.
3.   States which are members of a subregional or regional fisheries management organization or participants in a subregional or regional fisheries management arrangement shall, individually or jointly, request the fishing entities referred to in article 1, paragraph 3, which have fishing vessels in the relevant area to cooperate fully with such organization or arrangement in implementing the conservation and management measures it

has established, with a view to having such measures applied de facto as extensively as possible to fishing activities in the relevant area. Such fishing entities shall enjoy benefits from participation in the fishery commensurate with their commitment to comply with conservation and management measures in respect of the stocks.

4.   States which are members of such organization or participants in such arrangement shall exchange information with respect to the activities of fishing vessels flying the flags of States which are neither members of the organization nor participants in the arrangement and which are engaged in fishing operations for the relevant stocks. They shall take measures consistent with this Agreement and international law to deter activities of such vessels which undermine the effectiveness of subregional or regional conservation and management measures.

PART V

DUTIES OF THE FLAG STATE

Article 18
Duties of the flag State

1.   A State whose vessels fish on the high seas shall take such measures as may be necessary to ensure that vessels flying its flag comply with subregional and regional conservation and management measures and that such vessels do not engage in any activity which undermines the effectiveness of such measures.

2.   A State shall authorize the use of vessels flying its flag for fishing on the high seas only where it is able to exercise effectively its responsibilities in respect of such vessels under the Convention and this Agreement.

3.   Measures to be taken by a State in respect of vessels flying its flag shall include:

    (a)   control of such vessels on the high seas by means of fishing licences, authorizations or permits, in accordance with any applicable procedures agreed at the subregional, regional or global level;

    (b)   establishment of regulations:

        (i)   to apply terms and conditions to the licence, authorization or permit sufficient to fulfil any subregional, regional or global obligations of the flag State;

        (ii)   to prohibit fishing on the high seas by vessels which are not duly licensed or authorized to fish, or fishing on the high seas by vessels otherwise than in accordance with the terms and conditions of a licence, authorization or permit;

        (iii)   to require vessels fishing on the high seas to carry the licence, authorization or permit on board at all times and to produce it on demand for inspection by a duly authorized person; and

        (iv)   to ensure that vessels flying its flag do not conduct unauthorized fishing within areas under the national jurisdiction of other States;

    (c)   establishment of a national record of fishing vessels authorized to fish on the high seas and provision of access to the information contained in that record on request by directly interested States, taking into account any national laws of the flag State regarding the release of such information;

(d)   requirements for marking of fishing vessels and fishing gear for identification in accordance with uniform and internationally recognizable vessel and gear marking systems, such as the Food and Agriculture Organization of the United Nations Standard Specifications for the Marking and Identification of Fishing Vessels;

(e)   requirements for recording and timely reporting of vessel position, catch of target and non-target species, fishing effort and other relevant fisheries data in accordance with subregional, regional and global standards for collection of such data;

(f)   requirements for verifying the catch of target and non-target species through such means as observer programmes, inspection schemes, unloading reports, supervision of transshipment and monitoring of landed catches and market statistics;

(g)   monitoring, control and surveillance of such vessels, their fishing operations and related activities by, *inter alia*:

(i)   the implementation of national inspection schemes and subregional and regional schemes for cooperation in enforcement pursuant to articles 21 and 22, including requirements for such vessels to permit access by duly authorized inspectors from other States;

(ii)   the implementation of national observer programmes and subregional and regional observer programmes in which the flag State is a participant, including requirements for such vessels to permit access by observers from other States to carry out the functions agreed under the programmes; and

(iii)   the development and implementation of vessel monitoring systems, including, as appropriate, satellite transmitter systems, in accordance with any national programmes and those which have been subregionally, regionally or globally agreed among the States concerned;

(h)   regulation of transshipment on the high seas to ensure that the effectiveness of conservation and management measures is not undermined; and

(i)   regulation of fishing activities to ensure compliance with subregional, regional or global measures, including those aimed at minimizing catches of non-target species.

4.   Where there is a subregionally, regionally or globally agreed system of monitoring, control and surveillance in effect, States shall ensure that the measures they impose on vessels flying their flag are compatible with that system.

PART VI

COMPLIANCE AND ENFORCEMENT

Article 19
Compliance and enforcement by the flag State

1.   A State shall ensure compliance by vessels flying its flag with subregional and regional conservation and management measures for straddling fish stocks and highly migratory fish stocks. To this end, that State shall:

(a)   enforce such measures irrespective of where violations occur;

(b)   investigate immediately and fully any alleged violation of subregional or regional conservation and management measures, which may include the physical inspection of the vessels concerned, and report promptly to the State alleging the violation and the relevant subregional or regional organization or arrangement on the progress and outcome of the investigation;

(c)   require any vessel flying its flag to give information to the investigating authority regarding vessel position, catches, fishing gear, fishing operations and related activities in the area of an alleged violation;

(d)   if satisfied that sufficient evidence is available in respect of an alleged violation, refer the case to its authorities with a view to instituting proceedings without delay in accordance with its laws and, where appropriate, detain the vessel concerned; and

(e)   ensure that, where it has been established, in accordance with its laws, a vessel has been involved in the commission of a serious violation of such measures, the vessel does not engage in fishing operations on the high seas until such time as all outstanding sanctions imposed by the flag State in respect of the violation have been complied with.

2.   All investigations and judicial proceedings shall be carried out expeditiously. Sanctions applicable in respect of violations shall be adequate in severity to be effective in securing compliance and to discourage violations wherever they occur and shall deprive offenders of the benefits accruing from their illegal activities. Measures applicable in respect of masters and other officers of fishing vessels shall include provisions which may permit, *inter alia*, refusal, withdrawal or suspension of authorizations to serve as masters or officers on such vessels.

Article 20
International cooperation in enforcement

1.   States shall cooperate, either directly or through subregional or regional fisheries management organizations or arrangements, to ensure compliance with and enforcement of subregional and regional conservation and management measures for straddling fish stocks and highly migratory fish stocks.

2.   A flag State conducting an investigation of an alleged violation of conservation and management measures for straddling fish stocks or highly migratory fish stocks may request the assistance of any other State whose cooperation may be useful in the conduct of that investigation. All States shall endeavour to meet reasonable requests made by a flag State in connection with such investigations.

3.   A flag State may undertake such investigations directly, in cooperation with other interested States or through the relevant subregional or regional fisheries management organization or arrangement. Information

on the progress and outcome of the investigations shall be provided to all States having an interest in, or affected by, the alleged violation.

4.   States shall assist each other in identifying vessels reported to have engaged in activities undermining the effectiveness of subregional, regional or global conservation and management measures.

5.   States shall, to the extent permitted by national laws and regulations, establish arrangements for making available to prosecuting authorities in other States evidence relating to alleged violations of such measures.

6.   Where there are reasonable grounds for believing that a vessel on the high seas has been engaged in unauthorized fishing within an area under the jurisdiction of a coastal State, the flag State of that vessel, at the request of the coastal State concerned, shall immediately and fully investigate the matter.   The flag State shall cooperate with the coastal State in taking appropriate enforcement action in such cases and may authorize the relevant authorities of the coastal State to board and inspect the vessel on the high seas.   This paragraph is without prejudice to article 111 of the Convention.

7.   States Parties which are members of a subregional or regional fisheries management organization or participants in a subregional or regional fisheries management arrangement may take action in accordance with international law, including through recourse to subregional or regional procedures established for this purpose, to deter vessels which have engaged in activities which undermine the effectiveness of or otherwise violate the conservation and management measures established by that organization or arrangement from fishing on the high seas in the subregion or region until such time as appropriate action is taken by the flag State.

Article 21
Subregional and regional cooperation in enforcement

1.   In any high seas area covered by a subregional or regional fisheries management organization or arrangement, a State Party which is a member of such organization or a participant in such arrangement may, through its duly authorized inspectors, board and inspect, in accordance with paragraph 2, fishing vessels flying the flag of another State Party to this Agreement, whether or not such State Party is also a member of the organization or a participant in the arrangement, for the purpose of ensuring compliance with conservation and management measures for straddling fish stocks and highly migratory fish stocks established by that organization or arrangement.

2.   States shall establish, through subregional or regional fisheries management organizations or arrangements, procedures for boarding and inspection pursuant to paragraph 1, as well as procedures to implement other provisions of this article.   Such procedures shall be consistent with this article and the basic procedures set out in article 22 and shall not discriminate against non-members of the organization or non-participants in the arrangement.   Boarding and inspection as well as any subsequent enforcement action shall be conducted in accordance with such procedures. States shall give due publicity to procedures established pursuant to this paragraph.

3.   If, within two years of the adoption of this Agreement, any organization or arrangement has not established such procedures, boarding and inspection pursuant to paragraph 1, as well as any subsequent enforcement action, shall, pending the establishment of such procedures, be conducted in accordance with this article and the basic procedures set out in article 22.

4.   Prior to taking action under this article, inspecting States shall, either directly or through the relevant subregional or regional fisheries management organization or arrangement, inform all States whose vessels

fish on the high seas in the subregion or region of the form of identification issued to their duly authorized inspectors. The vessels used for boarding and inspection shall be clearly marked and identifiable as being on government service. At the time of becoming a Party to this Agreement, a State shall designate an appropriate authority to receive notifications pursuant to this article and shall give due publicity of such designation through the relevant subregional or regional fisheries management organization or arrangement.

5.   Where, following a boarding and inspection, there are clear grounds for believing that a vessel has engaged in any activity contrary to the conservation and management measures referred to in paragraph 1, the inspecting State shall, where appropriate, secure evidence and shall promptly notify the flag State of the alleged violation.

6.   The flag State shall respond to the notification referred to in paragraph 5 within three working days of its receipt, or such other period as may be prescribed in procedures established in accordance with paragraph 2, and shall either:

        (a)   fulfil, without delay, its obligations under article 19 to investigate and, if evidence so warrants, take enforcement action with respect to the vessel, in which case it shall promptly inform the inspecting State of the results of the investigation and of any enforcement action taken; or

        (b)   authorize the inspecting State to investigate.

7.   Where the flag State authorizes the inspecting State to investigate an alleged violation, the inspecting State shall, without delay, communicate the results of that investigation to the flag State. The flag State shall, if evidence so warrants, fulfil its obligations to take enforcement action with respect to the vessel. Alternatively, the flag State may authorize the inspecting State to take such enforcement action as the flag State may specify with respect to the vessel, consistent with the rights and obligations of the flag State under this Agreement.

8.   Where, following boarding and inspection, there are clear grounds for believing that a vessel has committed a serious violation, and the flag State has either failed to respond or failed to take action as required under paragraphs 6 or 7, the inspectors may remain on board and secure evidence and may require the master to assist in further investigation including, where appropriate, by bringing the vessel without delay to the nearest appropriate port, or to such other port as may be specified in procedures established in accordance with paragraph 2. The inspecting State shall immediately inform the flag State of the name of the port to which the vessel is to proceed. The inspecting State and the flag State and, as appropriate, the port State shall take all necessary steps to ensure the well-being of the crew regardless of their nationality.

9.   The inspecting State shall inform the flag State and the relevant organization or the participants in the relevant arrangement of the results of any further investigation.

10.   The inspecting State shall require its inspectors to observe generally accepted international regulations, procedures and practices relating to the safety of the vessel and the crew, minimize interference with fishing operations and, to the extent practicable, avoid action which would adversely affect the quality of the catch on board. The inspecting State shall ensure that boarding and inspection is not conducted in a manner that would constitute harassment of any fishing vessel.

11.   For the purposes of this article, a serious violation means:

        (a)   fishing without a valid licence, authorization or permit issued by the flag State in accordance with article 18, paragraph 3 (a);

        (b)   failing to maintain accurate records of catch and catch-related data, as required by the relevant subregional or regional fisheries management organization or arrangement, or serious misreporting of catch, contrary to the catch reporting requirements of such organization or arrangement;

(c)   fishing in a closed area, fishing during a closed season or fishing without, or after attainment of, a quota established by the relevant subregional or regional fisheries management organization or arrangement;

(d)   directed fishing for a stock which is subject to a moratorium or for which fishing is prohibited;

(e)   using prohibited fishing gear;

(f)   falsifying or concealing the markings, identity or registration of a fishing vessel;

(g)   concealing, tampering with or disposing of evidence relating to an investigation;

(h)   multiple violations which together constitute a serious disregard of conservation and management measures; or

(i)   such other violations as may be specified in procedures established by the relevant subregional or regional fisheries management organization or arrangement.

12.   Notwithstanding the other provisions of this article, the flag State may, at any time, take action to fulfil its obligations under article 19 with respect to an alleged violation. Where the vessel is under the direction of the inspecting State, the inspecting State shall, at the request of the flag State, release the vessel to the flag State along with full information on the progress and outcome of its investigation.

13.   This article is without prejudice to the right of the flag State to take any measures, including proceedings to impose penalties, according to its laws.

14.   This article applies mutatis mutandis to boarding and inspection by a State Party which is a member of a subregional or regional fisheries management organization or a participant in a subregional or regional fisheries management arrangement and which has clear grounds for believing that a fishing vessel flying the flag of another State Party has engaged in any activity contrary to relevant conservation and management measures referred to in paragraph 1 in the high seas area covered by such organization or arrangement, and such vessel has subsequently, during the same fishing trip, entered into an area under the national jurisdiction of the inspecting State.

15.   Where a subregional or regional fisheries management organization or arrangement has established an alternative mechanism which effectively discharges the obligation under this Agreement of its members or participants to ensure compliance with the conservation and management measures established by the organization or arrangement, members of such organization or participants in such arrangement may agree to limit the application of paragraph 1 as between themselves in respect of the conservation and management measures which have been established in the relevant high seas area.

16.   Action taken by States other than the flag State in respect of vessels having engaged in activities contrary to subregional or regional conservation and management measures shall be proportionate to the seriousness of the violation.

17.   Where there are reasonable grounds for suspecting that a fishing vessel on the high seas is without nationality, a State may board and inspect the vessel. Where evidence so warrants, the State may take such action as may be appropriate in accordance with international law.

18.   States shall be liable for damage or loss attributable to them arising from action taken pursuant to this article when such action is unlawful or exceeds that reasonably required in the light of available information to implement the provisions of this article.

Article 22
Basic procedures for boarding and inspection
pursuant to article 21

1.   The inspecting State shall ensure that its duly authorized inspectors:
(a)   present credentials to the master of the vessel and produce a copy of the text of the relevant conservation and management measures or rules and regulations in force in the high seas area in question pursuant to those measures;
(b)   initiate notice to the flag State at the time of the boarding and inspection;
(c)   do not interfere with the master's ability to communicate with the authorities of the flag State during the boarding and inspection;
(d)   provide a copy of a report on the boarding and inspection to the master and to the authorities of the flag State, noting therein any objection or statement which the master wishes to have included in the report;
(e)   promptly leave the vessel following completion of the inspection if they find no evidence of a serious violation; and
(f)   avoid the use of force except when and to the degree necessary to ensure the safety of the inspectors and where the inspectors are obstructed in the execution of their duties. The degree of force used shall not exceed that reasonably required in the circumstances.
2.   The duly authorized inspectors of an inspecting State shall have the authority to inspect the vessel, its licence, gear, equipment, records, facilities, fish and fish products and any relevant documents necessary to verify compliance with the relevant conservation and management measures.
3.   The flag State shall ensure that vessel masters:
(a)   accept and facilitate prompt and safe boarding by the inspectors;
(b)   cooperate with and assist in the inspection of the vessel conducted pursuant to these procedures;
(c)   do not obstruct, intimidate or interfere with the inspectors in the performance of their duties;
(d)   allow the inspectors to communicate with the authorities of the flag State and the inspecting State during the boarding and inspection;
(e)   provide reasonable facilities, including, where appropriate, food and accommodation, to the inspectors; and
(f)   facilitate safe disembarkation by the inspectors.
4.   In the event that the master of a vessel refuses to accept boarding and inspection in accordance with this article and article 21, the flag State shall, except in circumstances where, in accordance with generally accepted international regulations, procedures and practices relating to safety at sea, it is necessary to delay the boarding and inspection, direct the master of the vessel to submit immediately to boarding and inspection and, if the master does not comply with such direction, shall suspend the vessel's authorization to fish and order the vessel to return immediately to port. The flag State shall advise the inspecting State of the action it has taken when the circumstances referred to in this paragraph arise.

Article 23
Measures taken by a port State

1.   A port State has the right and the duty to take measures, in accordance with international law, to promote the effectiveness of subregional, regional and global conservation and management measures. When taking such measures a port State shall not discriminate in form or in fact against the vessels of any State.
2.   A port State may, *inter alia*, inspect documents, fishing gear and catch on board fishing vessels, when such vessels are voluntarily in its ports or at its offshore terminals.
3.   States may adopt regulations empowering the relevant national authorities to prohibit landings and transshipments where it has been established that the catch has been taken in a manner which undermines the effectiveness of subregional, regional or global conservation and management measures on the high seas.
4.   Nothing in this article affects the exercise by States of their sovereignty over ports in their territory in accordance with international law.

PART VII

REQUIREMENTS OF DEVELOPING STATES

Article 24
Recognition of the special requirements of developing States

1.   States shall give full recognition to the special requirements of developing States in relation to conservation and management of straddling fish stocks and highly migratory fish stocks and development of fisheries for such stocks. To this end, States shall, either directly or through the United Nations Development Programme, the Food and Agriculture Organization of the United Nations and other specialized agencies, the Global Environment Facility, the Commission on Sustainable Development and other appropriate international and regional organizations and bodies, provide assistance to developing States.
2.   In giving effect to the duty to cooperate in the establishment of conservation and management measures for straddling fish stocks and highly migratory fish stocks, States shall take into account the special requirements of developing States, in particular:
    (a)   the vulnerability of developing States which are dependent on the exploitation of living marine resources, including for meeting the nutritional requirements of their populations or parts thereof;
    (b)   the need to avoid adverse impacts on, and ensure access to fisheries by, subsistence, small-scale and artisanal fishers and women fishworkers, as well as indigenous people in developing States, particularly small island developing States; and
    (c)   the need to ensure that such measures do not result in transferring, directly or indirectly, a disproportionate burden of conservation action onto developing States.

Article 25
Forms of cooperation with developing States

1.   States shall cooperate, either directly or through subregional, regional or global organizations:
      (a)   to enhance the ability of developing States, in particular the least-developed among them and small island developing States, to conserve and manage straddling fish stocks and highly migratory fish stocks and to develop their own fisheries for such stocks;
      (b)   to assist developing States, in particular the least-developed among them and small island developing States, to enable them to participate in high seas fisheries for such stocks, including facilitating access to such fisheries subject to articles 5 and 11; and
      (c)   to facilitate the participation of developing States in subregional and regional fisheries management organizations and arrangements.
2.   Cooperation with developing States for the purposes set out in this article shall include the provision of financial assistance, assistance relating to human resources development, technical assistance, transfer of technology, including through joint venture arrangements, and advisory and consultative services.
3.   Such assistance shall, *inter alia*, be directed specifically towards:
      (a)   improved conservation and management of straddling fish stocks and highly migratory fish stocks through collection, reporting, verification, exchange and analysis of fisheries data and related information;
      (b)   stock assessment and scientific research; and
      (c)   monitoring, control, surveillance, compliance and enforcement, including training and capacity-building at the local level, development and funding of national and regional observer programmes and access to technology and equipment.

Article 26
Special assistance in the implementation of this Agreement

1.   States shall cooperate to establish special funds to assist developing States in the implementation of this Agreement, including assisting developing States to meet the costs involved in any proceedings for the settlement of disputes to which they may be parties.
2.   States and international organizations should assist developing States in establishing new subregional or regional fisheries management organizations or arrangements, or in strengthening existing organizations or arrangements, for the conservation and management of straddling fish stocks and highly migratory fish stocks.

PART VIII

PEACEFUL SETTLEMENT OF DISPUTES

Article 27
Obligation to settle disputes by peaceful means

      States have the obligation to settle their disputes by negotiation, inquiry, mediation, conciliation, arbitration, judicial settlement, resort to regional agencies or arrangements, or other peaceful means of their own choice.

Article 28
Prevention of disputes

States shall cooperate in order to prevent disputes. To this end, States shall agree on efficient and expeditious decision-making procedures within subregional and regional fisheries management organizations and arrangements and shall strengthen existing decision-making procedures as necessary.

Article 29
Disputes of a technical nature

Where a dispute concerns a matter of a technical nature, the States concerned may refer the dispute to an ad hoc expert panel established by them. The panel shall confer with the States concerned and shall endeavour to resolve the dispute expeditiously without recourse to binding procedures for the settlement of disputes.

Article 30
Procedures for the settlement of disputes

1.   The provisions relating to the settlement of disputes set out in Part XV of the Convention apply *mutatis mutandis* to any dispute between States Parties to this Agreement concerning the interpretation or application of this Agreement, whether or not they are also Parties to the Convention.

2.   The provisions relating to the settlement of disputes set out in Part XV of the Convention apply *mutatis mutandis* to any dispute between States Parties to this Agreement concerning the interpretation or application of a subregional, regional or global fisheries agreement relating to straddling fish stocks or highly migratory fish stocks to which they are parties, including any dispute concerning the conservation and management of such stocks, whether or not they are also Parties to the Convention.

3.   Any procedure accepted by a State Party to this Agreement and the Convention pursuant to article 287 of the Convention shall apply to the settlement of disputes under this Part, unless that State Party, when signing, ratifying or acceding to this Agreement, or at any time thereafter, has accepted another procedure pursuant to article 287 for the settlement of disputes under this Part.

4.   A State Party to this Agreement which is not a Party to the Convention, when signing, ratifying or acceding to this Agreement, or at any time thereafter, shall be free to choose, by means of a written declaration, one or more of the means set out in article 287, paragraph 1, of the Convention for the settlement of disputes under this Part. Article 287 shall apply to such a declaration, as well as to any dispute to which such State is a party which is not covered by a declaration in force. For the purposes of conciliation and arbitration in accordance with Annexes V, VII and VIII to the Convention, such State shall be entitled to nominate conciliators, arbitrators and experts to be included in the lists referred to in Annex V, article 2, Annex VII, article 2, and Annex VIII, article 2, for the settlement of disputes under this Part.

5.   Any court or tribunal to which a dispute has been submitted under this Part shall apply the relevant provisions of the Convention, of this Agreement and of any relevant subregional, regional or global fisheries agreement, as well as generally accepted standards for the conservation and management of living marine resources and other rules of international law not incompatible with the Convention, with a view to ensuring the

conservation of the straddling fish stocks and highly migratory fish stocks concerned.

Article 31
Provisional measures

1.　　Pending the settlement of a dispute in accordance with this Part, the parties to the dispute shall make every effort to enter into provisional arrangements of a practical nature.
2.　　Without prejudice to article 290 of the Convention, the court or tribunal to which the dispute has been submitted under this Part may prescribe any provisional measures which it considers appropriate under the circumstances to preserve the respective rights of the parties to the dispute or to prevent damage to the stocks in question, as well as in the circumstances referred to in article 7, paragraph 5, and article 16, paragraph 2.
3.　　A State Party to this Agreement which is not a Party to the Convention may declare that, notwithstanding article 290, paragraph 5, of the Convention, the International Tribunal for the Law of the Sea shall not be entitled to prescribe, modify or revoke provisional measures without the agreement of such State.

Article 32
Limitations on applicability of procedures for the settlement of disputes

Article 297, paragraph 3, of the Convention applies also to this Agreement.

PART IX

NON-PARTIES TO THIS AGREEMENT

Article 33
Non-parties to this Agreement

1.　　States Parties shall encourage non-parties to this Agreement to become parties thereto and to adopt laws and regulations consistent with its provisions.
2.　　States Parties shall take measures consistent with this Agreement and international law to deter the activities of vessels flying the flag of non-parties which undermine the effective implementation of this Agreement.

PART X

GOOD FAITH AND ABUSE OF RIGHTS

Article 34
Good faith and abuse of rights

States Parties shall fulfil in good faith the obligations assumed under this Agreement and shall exercise the rights recognized in this Agreement in a manner which would not constitute an abuse of right.

PART XI

RESPONSIBILITY AND LIABILITY

Article 35
Responsibility and liability

States Parties are liable in accordance with international law for damage or loss attributable to them in regard to this Agreement.

PART XII

REVIEW CONFERENCE

Article 36
Review conference

1.   Four years after the date of entry into force of this Agreement, the Secretary-General of the United Nations shall convene a conference with a view to assessing the effectiveness of this Agreement in securing the conservation and management of straddling fish stocks and highly migratory fish stocks. The Secretary-General shall invite to the conference all States Parties and those States and entities which are entitled to become parties to this Agreement as well as those intergovernmental and non-governmental organizations entitled to participate as observers.
2.   The conference shall review and assess the adequacy of the provisions of this Agreement and, if necessary, propose means of strengthening the substance and methods of implementation of those provisions in order better to address any continuing problems in the conservation and management of straddling fish stocks and highly migratory fish stocks.

PART XIII

FINAL PROVISIONS

Article 37
Signature

This Agreement shall be open for signature by all States and the other entities referred to in article 1, paragraph 2(b), and shall remain open for signature at United Nations Headquarters for twelve months from the fourth of December 1995.

Article 38
Ratification

This Agreement is subject to ratification by States and the other entities referred to in article 1, paragraph 2(b). The instruments of ratification shall be deposited with the Secretary-General of the United Nations.

Article 39
Accession

This Agreement shall remain open for accession by States and the other entities referred to in article 1, paragraph 2(b). The instruments of accession shall be deposited with the Secretary-General of the United Nations.

Article 40
Entry into force

1.   This Agreement shall enter into force 30 days after the date of deposit of the thirtieth instrument of ratification or accession.
2.   For each State or entity which ratifies the Agreement or accedes thereto after the deposit of the thirtieth instrument of ratification or accession, this Agreement shall enter into force on the thirtieth day following the deposit of its instrument of ratification or accession.

Article 41
Provisional application

1.   This Agreement shall be applied provisionally by a State or entity which consents to its provisional application by so notifying the depositary in writing. Such provisional application shall become effective from the date of receipt of the notification.
2.   Provisional application by a State or entity shall terminate upon the entry into force of this Agreement for that State or entity or upon notification by that State or entity to the depositary in writing of its intention to terminate provisional application.

Article 42
Reservations and exceptions

No reservations or exceptions may be made to this Agreement.

Article 43
Declarations and statements

Article 42 does not preclude a State or entity, when signing, ratifying or acceding to this Agreement, from making declarations or statements, however phrased or named, with a view, *inter alia*, to the harmonization of its laws and regulations with the provisions of this Agreement, provided that such declarations or statements do not purport to exclude or to modify the legal effect of the provisions of this Agreement in their application to that State or entity.

Article 44
Relation to other agreements

1.   This Agreement shall not alter the rights and obligations of States Parties which arise from other agreements compatible with this Agreement and which do not affect the enjoyment by other States Parties of their rights or the performance of their obligations under this Agreement.
2.   Two or more States Parties may conclude agreements modifying or suspending the operation of provisions of this Agreement, applicable solely to the relations between them, provided that such agreements do not relate to a provision derogation from which is incompatible with the effective execution of the object and purpose of this Agreement, and provided further that such agreements shall not affect the application of the basic principles embodied herein, and that the provisions of such agreements do not affect the enjoyment by other States Parties of their rights or the performance of their obligations under this Agreement.

3. States Parties intending to conclude an agreement referred to in paragraph 2 shall notify the other States Parties through the depositary of this Agreement of their intention to conclude the agreement and of the modification or suspension for which it provides.

Article 45
Amendment

1. A State Party may, by written communication addressed to the Secretary-General of the United Nations, propose amendments to this Agreement and request the convening of a conference to consider such proposed amendments. The Secretary-General shall circulate such communication to all States Parties. If, within six months from the date of the circulation of the communication, not less than one half of the States Parties reply favourably to the request, the Secretary-General shall convene the conference.
2. The decision-making procedure applicable at the amendment conference convened pursuant to paragraph 1 shall be the same as that applicable at the United Nations Conference on Straddling Fish Stocks and Highly Migratory Fish Stocks, unless otherwise decided by the conference. The conference should make every effort to reach agreement on any amendments by way of consensus and there should be no voting on them until all efforts at consensus have been exhausted.
3. Once adopted, amendments to this Agreement shall be open for signature at United Nations Headquarters by States Parties for twelve months from the date of adoption, unless otherwise provided in the amendment itself.
4. Articles 38, 39, 47 and 50 apply to all amendments to this Agreement.
5. Amendments to this Agreement shall enter into force for the States Parties ratifying or acceding to them on the thirtieth day following the deposit of instruments of ratification or accession by two thirds of the States Parties. Thereafter, for each State Party ratifying or acceding to an amendment after the deposit of the required number of such instruments, the amendment shall enter into force on the thirtieth day following the deposit of its instrument of ratification or accession.
6. An amendment may provide that a smaller or a larger number of ratifications or accessions shall be required for its entry into force than are required by this article.
7. A State which becomes a Party to this Agreement after the entry into force of amendments in accordance with paragraph 5 shall, failing an expression of a different intention by that State:
    (a) be considered as a Party to this Agreement as so amended; and
    (b) be considered as a Party to the unamended Agreement in relation to any State Party not bound by the amendment.

Article 46
Denunciation

1. A State Party may, by written notification addressed to the Secretary-General of the United Nations, denounce this Agreement and may indicate its reasons. Failure to indicate reasons shall not affect the validity of the denunciation. The denunciation shall take effect one year after the date of receipt of the notification, unless the notification specifies a later date.

2.   The denunciation shall not in any way affect the duty of any State Party to fulfil any obligation embodied in this Agreement to which it would be subject under international law independently of this Agreement.

Article 47
Participation by international organizations

1.   In cases where an international organization referred to in Annex IX, article 1, of the Convention does not have competence over all the matters governed by this Agreement, Annex IX to the Convention shall apply *mutatis mutandis* to participation by such international organization in this Agreement, except that the following provisions of that Annex shall not apply:

(a)   article 2, first sentence; and
(b)   article 3, paragraph 1.

2.   In cases where an international organization referred to in Annex IX, article 1, of the Convention has competence over all the matters governed by this Agreement, the following provisions shall apply to participation by such international organization in this Agreement:

(a)   at the time of signature or accession, such international organization shall make a declaration stating:

(i)   that it has competence over all the matters governed by this Agreement;

(ii)   that, for this reason, its member States shall not become States Parties, except in respect of their territories for which the international organization has no responsibility; and

(iii)   that it accepts the rights and obligations of States under this Agreement;

(b) participation of such an international organization shall in no case confer any rights under this Agreement on member States of the international organization;

(c) in the event of a conflict between the obligations of an international organization under this Agreement and its obligations under the agreement establishing the international organization or any acts relating to it, the obligations under this Agreement shall prevail.

Article 48
Annexes

1.   The Annexes form an integral part of this Agreement and, unless expressly provided otherwise, a reference to this Agreement or to one of its Parts includes a reference to the Annexes relating thereto.

2.   The Annexes may be revised from time to time by States Parties. Such revisions shall be based on scientific and technical considerations. Notwithstanding the provisions of article 45, if a revision to an Annex is adopted by consensus at a meeting of States Parties, it shall be incorporated in this Agreement and shall take effect from the date of its adoption or from such other date as may be specified in the revision. If a revision to an Annex is not adopted by consensus at such a meeting, the amendment procedures set out in article 45 shall apply.

Article 49
Depositary

The Secretary-General of the United Nations shall be the depositary of this Agreement and any amendments or revisions thereto.

Article 50
Authentic texts

The Arabic, Chinese, English, French, Russian and Spanish texts of this Agreement are equally authentic.

IN WITNESS WHEREOF, the undersigned Plenipotentiaries, being duly authorized thereto, have signed this Agreement.

OPENED FOR SIGNATURE at New York, this fourth day of December, one thousand nine hundred and ninety-five, in a single original, in the Arabic, Chinese, English, French, Russian and Spanish languages.

ANNEX I

STANDARD REQUIREMENTS FOR THE COLLECTION AND SHARING OF DATA

Article 1
General principles

1.   The timely collection, compilation and analysis of data are fundamental to the effective conservation and management of straddling fish stocks and highly migratory fish stocks. To this end, data from fisheries for these stocks on the high seas and those in areas under national jurisdiction are required and should be collected and compiled in such a way as to enable statistically meaningful analysis for the purposes of fishery resource conservation and management. These data include catch and fishing effort statistics and other fishery-related information, such as vessel-related and other data for standardizing fishing effort. Data collected should also include information on non-target and associated or dependent species. All data should be verified to ensure accuracy. Confidentiality of non-aggregated data shall be maintained. The dissemination of such data shall be subject to the terms on which they have been provided.
2.   Assistance, including training as well as financial and technical assistance, shall be provided to developing States in order to build capacity in the field of conservation and management of living marine resources. Assistance should focus on enhancing capacity to implement data collection and verification, observer programmes, data analysis and research projects supporting stock assessments. The fullest possible involvement of developing State scientists and managers in conservation and management of straddling fish stocks and highly migratory fish stocks should be promoted.

Article 2
Principles of data collection, compilation and exchange

The following general principles should be considered in defining the parameters for collection, compilation and exchange of data from fishing operations for straddling fish stocks and highly migratory fish stocks:
(a) States should ensure that data are collected from vessels flying their flag on fishing activities according to the operational characteristics of each fishing method (e.g., each individual tow for trawl, each set for long-line and purse-seine, each school fished for pole-and-line and each day fished for troll) and in sufficient detail to facilitate effective stock assessment;
(b) States should ensure that fishery data are verified through an appropriate system;
(c) States should compile fishery-related and other supporting scientific data and provide them in an agreed format and in a timely manner to the relevant subregional or regional fisheries management organization or arrangement where one exists. Otherwise, States should cooperate to exchange data either directly or through such other cooperative mechanisms as may be agreed among them;
(d) States should agree, within the framework of subregional or regional fisheries management organizations or arrangements, or otherwise, on the specification of data and the format in which they are to be provided, in accordance with this Annex and taking into account the nature of the stocks and the fisheries for those stocks in the region. Such organizations or arrangements should request non-members or non-participants to provide data concerning relevant fishing activities by vessels flying their flag;

(e) such organizations or arrangements shall compile data and make them available in a timely manner and in an agreed format to all interested States under the terms and conditions established by the organization or arrangement; and
(f) scientists of the flag State and from the relevant subregional or regional fisheries management organization or arrangement should analyse the data separately or jointly, as appropriate.

Article 3
Basic fishery data

1.   States shall collect and make available to the relevant subregional or regional fisheries management organization or arrangement the following types of data in sufficient detail to facilitate effective stock assessment in accordance with agreed procedures:
(a) time series of catch and effort statistics by fishery and fleet;
(b) total catch in number, nominal weight, or both, by species (both target and non-target) as is appropriate to each fishery. [Nominal weight is defined by the Food and Agriculture Organization of the United Nations as the live-weight equivalent of the landings];
(c) discard statistics, including estimates where necessary, reported as number or nominal weight by species, as is appropriate to each fishery;
(d) effort statistics appropriate to each fishing method; and
(e) fishing location, date and time fished and other statistics on fishing operations as appropriate.
2.   States shall also collect where appropriate and provide to the relevant subregional or regional fisheries management organization or arrangement information to support stock assessment, including:
(a) composition of the catch according to length, weight and sex;
(b) other biological information supporting stock assessments, such as information on age, growth, recruitment, distribution and stock identity; and
(c) other relevant research, including surveys of abundance, biomass surveys, hydro-acoustic surveys, research on environmental factors affecting stock abundance, and oceanographic and ecological studies.

Article 4
Vessel data and information

1.   States should collect the following types of vessel-related data for standardizing fleet composition and vessel fishing power and for converting between different measures of effort in the analysis of catch and effort data:
(a) vessel identification, flag and port of registry;
(b) vessel type;
(c) vessel specifications (e.g., material of construction, date built, registered length, gross registered tonnage, power of main engines, hold capacity and catch storage methods); and
(d) fishing gear description (e.g., types, gear specifications and quantity).
2.   The flag State will collect the following information:
(a) navigation and position fixing aids;
(b) communication equipment and international radio call sign; and
(c) crew size.

Article 5
Reporting

A State shall ensure that vessels flying its flag send to its national fisheries administration and, where agreed, to the relevant subregional or regional fisheries management organization or arrangement, logbook data on catch and effort, including data on fishing operations on the high seas, at sufficiently frequent intervals to meet national requirements and regional and international obligations. Such data shall be transmitted, where necessary, by radio, telex, facsimile or satellite transmission or by other means.

Article 6
Data verification

States or, as appropriate, subregional or regional fisheries management organizations or arrangements should establish mechanisms for verifying fishery data, such as:
  (a) position verification through vessel monitoring systems;
  (b) scientific observer programmes to monitor catch, effort, catch composition (target and non-target) and other details of fishing operations;
  (c) vessel trip, landing and transshipment reports; and
  (d) port sampling.

Article 7
Data exchange

1.   Data collected by flag States must be shared with other flag States and relevant coastal States through appropriate subregional or regional fisheries management organizations or arrangements. Such organizations or arrangements shall compile data and make them available in a timely manner and in an agreed format to all interested States under the terms and conditions established by the organization or arrangement, while maintaining confidentiality of non-aggregated data, and should, to the extent feasible, develop database systems which provide efficient access to data.
2.   At the global level, collection and dissemination of data should be effected through the Food and Agriculture Organization of the United Nations. Where a subregional or regional fisheries management organization or arrangement does not exist, that organization may also do the same at the subregional or regional level by arrangement with the States concerned.

ANNEX II

GUIDELINES FOR THE APPLICATION OF PRECAUTIONARY REFERENCE POINTS IN CONSERVATION AND MANAGEMENT OF STRADDLING FISH STOCKS AND HIGHLY MIGRATORY FISH STOCKS

1.   A precautionary reference point is an estimated value derived through an agreed scientific procedure, which corresponds to the state of the resource and of the fishery, and which can be used as a guide for fisheries management.

2.   Two types of precautionary reference points should be used: conservation, or limit, reference points and management, or target, reference points. Limit reference points set boundaries which are intended to constrain harvesting within safe biological limits within which the stocks can produce maximum sustainable yield. Target reference points are intended to meet management objectives.

3.   Precautionary reference points should be stock-specific to account, inter alia, for the reproductive capacity, the resilience of each stock and the characteristics of fisheries exploiting the stock, as well as other sources of mortality and major sources of uncertainty.

4.   Management strategies shall seek to maintain or restore populations of harvested stocks, and where necessary associated or dependent species, at levels consistent with previously agreed precautionary reference points. Such reference points shall be used to trigger pre-agreed conservation and management action. Management strategies shall include measures which can be implemented when precautionary reference points are approached.

5.   Fishery management strategies shall ensure that the risk of exceeding limit reference points is very low. If a stock falls below a limit reference point or is at risk of falling below such a reference point, conservation and management action should be initiated to facilitate stock recovery. Fishery management strategies shall ensure that target reference points are not exceeded on average.

6.   When information for determining reference points for a fishery is poor or absent, provisional reference points shall be set. Provisional reference points may be established by analogy to similar and better-known stocks. In such situations, the fishery shall be subject to enhanced monitoring so as to enable revision of provisional reference points as improved information becomes available.

7.   The fishing mortality rate which generates maximum sustainable yield should be regarded as a minimum standard for limit reference points. For stocks which are not overfished, fishery management strategies shall ensure that fishing mortality does not exceed that which corresponds to maximum sustainable yield, and that the biomass does not fall below a predefined threshold. For overfished stocks, the biomass which would produce maximum sustainable yield can serve as a rebuilding target.

II. Agreement to Promote Compliance with International Conservation and Management Measures by Fishing Vessels on the High Seas

Background

The problem of reflagging was first raised during the International Conference on Responsible Fishing in May 1992. The Declaration of Cancun adopted by that Conference called upon States "to take effective action, consistent with international law, to deter reflagging of fishing vessels as a means of avoiding compliance with applicable conservation and management rules for fishing activities on the high seas." A similar call for action was made by the United Nations Conference on Environment and Development in the context of Agenda 21 and by the FAO Technical Consultation on High Seas Fishing in September 1992. At its one hundred and second session in November 1992, the FAO Council agreed that the reflagging issue should be dealt with as a matter of urgency and mandated the FAO Secretariat to facilitate the negotiation of an international agreement on the "fast track".

The mandate given by the FAO Council in November 1992 gave rise to an unusually speedy negotiation process. An informal Group of Experts was convened in Rome in February 1993 to draw up a first tentative draft of an agreement. The draft was considered by the Committee on Fisheries at its twentieth session in Rome in March 1993, through an open-ended Working Group set up for that purpose. The text was then considered by the FAO Council at its one hundred and third session in June 1993, again through the mechanism of an open Technical Committee that met simultaneously with the full Council session. At that session, the Council agreed on the main lines of the draft agreement, but was unable, owing to the pressure of time, to reach full agreement on all provisions of the final text. The Council therefore asked the FAO Secretariat to continue informal consultations with FAO members with a view to resolving the outstanding issues. These informal consultations were held during the second session of the United Nations Conference on Straddling Fish Stocks and Highly Migratory Fish Stocks in New York in July 1993, as a result of which consensus was reached on the full text of the Agreement. Meanwhile the text had been circulated to all FAO members for comment, and those comments were taken into account during the sixty-first session of the FAO Committee on Constitutional and Legal Matters in October 1993 and during a final negotiating session of the open Technical Committee held during the one hundred and fourth session of the Council in November 1993.

At its twenty-seventh session, on 24 November 1993, the FAO Conference approved a new Agreement to Promote Compliance with International Conservation and Management Measures by Fishing Vessels on the High Seas, under article XIV of the FAO Constitution. Article XIV allows for international conventions or agreements of general application in the field of food and agriculture to be approved by the Conference and submitted to FAO members, associate members and eligible non-member

States for acceptance. In this context it is to be noted that the European Community has been a member of FAO since its admission in November 1991 and thus will be entitled to become a full party to the Agreement. In doing so, the Conference "acclaimed the agreement as a momentous achievement and a milestone in the international management of high seas". The Agreement, as stated in its Preamble, "will form an integral part of the Code of Conduct" for Responsible Fisheries. This is further confirmed in the Code of Conduct itself in article I.

The Agreement will enter into force on the date of deposit of the twenty-fifth instrument of acceptance.

Agreement to Promote Compliance with International Conservation and Management Measures by Fishing Vessels on the High Seas

Preamble

The Parties to this Agreement,

Recognizing that all States have the right for their nationals to engage in fishing on the high seas, subject to the relevant rules of international law, as reflected in the United Nations Convention on the Law of the Sea,

Further recognizing that, under international law as reflected in the United Nations Convention on the Law of the Sea, all States have the duty to take, or to cooperate with other States in taking, such measures for their respective nationals as may be necessary for the conservation of the living resources of the high seas,

Acknowledging the right and interest of all States to develop their fishing sectors in accordance with their national policies, and the need to promote cooperation with developing countries to enhance their capabilities to fulfil their obligations under this Agreement,

Recalling that Agenda 21, adopted by the United Nations Conference on Environment and Development, calls upon States to take effective action, consistent with international law, to deter reflagging of vessels by their nationals as a means of avoiding compliance with applicable conservation and management rules for fishing activities on the high seas,

Further recalling that the Declaration of Cancun, adopted by the International Conference on Responsible Fishing, also calls on States to take action in this respect,

Bearing in mind that under Agenda 21, States commit themselves to the conservation and sustainable use of marine living resources on the high seas,

Calling upon States which do not participate in global, regional or subregional fisheries organizations or arrangements to join or, as appropriate, to enter into understandings with such organizations or with parties to such organizations or arrangements with a view to achieving compliance with international conservation and management measures,

Conscious of the duties of every State to exercise effectively its jurisdiction and control over vessels flying its flag, including fishing vessels and vessels engaged in the transhipment of fish,

Mindful that the practice of flagging or reflagging fishing vessels as a means of avoiding compliance with international conservation and management measures for living marine resources, and the failure of flag States to fulfil their responsibilities with respect to fishing vessels entitled to fly their flag, are among the factors that seriously undermine the effectiveness of such measures,

Realizing that the objective of this Agreement can be achieved through specifying flag States' responsibility in respect of fishing vessels entitled to fly their flags and operating on the high seas, including the authorization by the flag State of such operations, as well as through strengthened international cooperation and increased transparency through the exchange of information on high seas fishing,

Noting that this Agreement will form an integral part of the International Code of Conduct for Responsible Fishing called for in the Declaration of Cancun,

Desiring to conclude an international agreement within the framework of the Food and Agriculture Organization of the United Nations, hereinafter referred to as FAO, under Article XIV of the FAO Constitution,

Have agreed as follows:

Article I
Definitions

For the purposes of this Agreement:
(a) "fishing vessel" means any vessel used or intended for use for the purposes of the commercial exploitation of living marine resources, including mother ships and any other vessels directly engaged in such fishing operations;
(b) "international conservation and management measures" means measures to conserve or manage one or more species of living marine resources that are adopted and applied in accordance with the relevant rules of international law as reflected in the 1982 United Nations Convention on the Law of the Sea. Such measures may be adopted either by global, regional or subregional fisheries organizations, subject to the rights and obligations of their members, or by treaties or other international agreements;
(c) "length" means
     (i)   for any fishing vessel built after 18 July 1982, 96 percent of the total length on a waterline at 85 percent of the least moulded depth measured from the top of the keel, or the length from the foreside of the stem to the axis of the rudder stock on that waterline, if that be greater. In ships designed with a rake of keel the waterline on which this length is measured shall be parallel to the designed waterline;
     (ii)   for any fishing vessel built before 18 July 1982, registered length as entered on the national register or other record of vessels;
(d) "record of fishing vessels" means a record of fishing vessels in which are recorded pertinent details of the fishing vessel. It may constitute a separate record for fishing vessels or form part of a general record of vessels;
(e) "regional economic integration organization" means a regional economic integration organization to which its member States have transferred competence over matters covered by this Agreement, including the authority to make decisions binding on its member States in respect of those matters;
(f) "vessels entitled to fly its flag" and "vessels entitled to fly the flag of a State", includes vessels entitled to fly the flag of a member State of a regional economic integration organization.

Article II
Application

1.   Subject to the following paragraphs of this Article, this Agreement shall apply to all fishing vessels that are used or intended for fishing on the high seas.
2.   A Party may exempt fishing vessels of less than 24 metres in length entitled to fly its flag from the application of this Agreement unless the Party determines that such an exemption would undermine the object and purpose of this Agreement, provided that such exemptions:
      (a) shall not be granted in respect of fishing vessels operating in fishing regions referred to in paragraph 3 below, other than

fishing vessels that are entitled to fly the flag of a coastal State of that fishing region; and
(b) shall not apply to the obligations undertaken by a Party under paragraph 1 of Article III, or paragraph 7 of Article VI of this Agreement.

3.   Without prejudice to the provisions of paragraph 2 above, in any fishing region where bordering coastal States have not yet declared exclusive economic zones, or equivalent zones of national jurisdiction over fisheries, such coastal States as are Parties to this Agreement may agree, either directly or through appropriate regional fisheries organizations, to establish a minimum length of fishing vessels below which this Agreement shall not apply in respect of fishing vessels flying the flag of any such coastal State and operating exclusively in such fishing region.

Article III
Flag State Responsibility

1.   (a) Each Party shall take such measures as may be necessary to ensure that fishing vessels entitled to fly its flag do not engage in any activity that undermines the effectiveness of international conservation and management measures.
      (b) In the event that a Party has, pursuant to paragraph 2 of Article II, granted an exemption for fishing vessels of less than 24 metres in length entitled to fly its flag from the application of other provisions of this Agreement, such Party shall nevertheless take effective measures in respect of any such fishing vessel that undermines the effectiveness of international conservation and management measures. These measures shall be such as to ensure that the fishing vessel ceases to engage in activities that undermine the effectiveness of the international conservation and management measures.

2.   In particular, no Party shall allow any fishing vessel entitled to fly its flag to be used for fishing on the high seas unless it has been authorized to be so used by the appropriate authority or authorities of that Party. A fishing vessel so authorized shall fish in accordance with the conditions of the authorization.

3.   No Party shall authorize any fishing vessel entitled to fly its flag to be used for fishing on the high seas unless the Party is satisfied that it is able, taking into account the links that exist between it and the fishing vessel concerned, to exercise effectively its responsibilities under this Agreement in respect of that fishing vessel.

4.   Where a fishing vessel that has been authorized to be used for fishing on the high seas by a Party ceases to be entitled to fly the flag of that Party, the authorization to fish on the high seas shall be deemed to have been cancelled.

5.   (a) No Party shall authorize any fishing vessel previously registered in the territory of another Party that has undermined the effectiveness of international conservation and management measures to be used for fishing on the high seas, unless it is satisfied that
          (i)   any period of suspension by another Party of an authorization for such fishing vessel to be used for fishing on the high seas has expired; and
          (ii)   no authorization for such fishing vessel to be used for fishing on the high seas has been withdrawn by another Party within the last three years.

(b) The provisions of subparagraph (a) above shall also apply in respect of fishing vessels previously registered in the territory of a State which is not a Party to this Agreement, provided that sufficient information is available to the Party concerned on the circumstances in which the authorization to fish was suspended or withdrawn.

(c) The provisions of subparagraphs (a) and (b) shall not apply where the ownership of the fishing vessel has subsequently changed, and the new owner has provided sufficient evidence demonstrating that the previous owner or operator has no further legal, beneficial or financial interest in, or control of, the fishing vessel.

(d) Notwithstanding the provisions of subparagraphs (a) and (b) above, a Party may authorize a fishing vessel, to which those subparagraphs would otherwise apply, to be used for fishing on the high seas, where the Party concerned, after having taken into account all relevant facts, including the circumstances in which the fishing authorization has been withdrawn by the other Party or State, has determined that to grant an authorization to use the vessel for fishing on the high seas would not undermine the object and purpose of this Agreement.

6.   Each Party shall ensure that all fishing vessels entitled to fly its flag that it has entered in the record maintained under Article IV are marked in such a way that they can be readily identified in accordance with generally accepted standards, such as the FAO Standard Specifications for the Marking and Identification of Fishing Vessels.

7.   Each Party shall ensure that each fishing vessel entitled to fly its flag shall provide it with such information on its operations as may be necessary to enable the Party to fulfil its obligations under this Agreement, including in particular information pertaining to the area of its fishing operations and to its catches and landings.

8.   Each Party shall take enforcement measures in respect of fishing vessels entitled to fly its flag which act in contravention of the provisions of this Agreement, including, where appropriate, making the contravention of such provisions an offence under national legislation. Sanctions applicable in respect of such contraventions shall be of sufficient gravity as to be effective in securing compliance with the requirements of this Agreement and to deprive offenders of the benefits accruing from their illegal activities. Such sanctions shall, for serious offences, include refusal, suspension or withdrawal of the authorization to fish on the high seas.

Article IV
Records of Fishing Vessels

Each Party shall, for the purposes of this Agreement, maintain a record of fishing vessels entitled to fly its flag and authorized to be used for fishing on the high seas, and shall take such measures as may be necessary to ensure that all such fishing vessels are entered in that record.

Article V
International Cooperation

1.   The Parties shall cooperate as appropriate in the implementation of this Agreement, and shall, in particular, exchange information, including evidentiary material, relating to activities of fishing vessels in order to assist the flag State in identifying those fishing vessels flying its flag reported to

have engaged in activities undermining international conservation and management measures, so as to fulfil its obligations under Article III.

2. When a fishing vessel is voluntarily in the port of a Party other than its flag State, that Party, where it has reasonable grounds for believing that the fishing vessel has been used for an activity that undermines the effectiveness of international conservation and management measures, shall promptly notify the flag State accordingly. Parties may make arrangements regarding the undertaking by port States of such investigatory measures as may be considered necessary to establish whether the fishing vessel has indeed been used contrary to the provisions of this Agreement.

3. The Parties shall, when and as appropriate, enter into cooperative agreements or arrangements of mutual assistance on a global, regional, subregional or bilateral basis so as to promote the achievement of the objectives of this Agreement.

Article VI
Exchange of Information

1. Each Party shall make readily available to FAO the following information with respect to each fishing vessel entered in the record required to be maintained under Article IV:
   (a) name of fishing vessel, registration number, previous names (if known), and port of registry;
   (b) previous flag (if any);
   (c) International Radio Call Sign (if any);
   (d) name and address of owner or owners;
   (e) where and when built;
   (f) type of vessel;
   (g) length.

2. Each Party shall, to the extent practicable, make available to FAO the following additional information with respect to each fishing vessel entered in the record required to be maintained under Article IV:
   (a) name and address of operator (manager) or operators (managers) (if any);
   (b) type of fishing method or methods;
   (c) moulded depth;
   (d) beam;
   (e) gross register tonnage;
   (f) power of main engine or engines.

3. Each Party shall promptly notify to FAO any modifications to the information listed in paragraphs 1 and 2 of this Article.

4. FAO shall circulate periodically the information provided under paragraphs 1, 2, and 3 of this Article to all Parties, and, on request, individually to any Party. FAO shall also, subject to any restrictions imposed by the Party concerned regarding the distribution of information, provide such information on request individually to any global, regional or subregional fisheries organization.

5. Each Party shall also promptly inform FAO of -
   (a) any additions to the record;
   (b) any deletions from the record by reason of -
      (i) the voluntary relinquishment or non-renewal of the fishing authorization by the fishing vessel owner or operator;
      (ii) the withdrawal of the fishing authorization issued in respect of the fishing vessel under paragraph 8 of Article III;

        (iii)   the fact that the fishing vessel concerned is no longer
                   entitled to fly its flag;
        (iv)   the scrapping, decommissioning or loss of the fishing
                   vessel concerned; or
        (v)   any other reason.

6.   Where information is given to FAO under paragraph 5 (b) above, the Party concerned shall specify which of the reasons listed in that paragraph is applicable.

7.   Each Party shall inform FAO of
      (a) any exemption it has granted under paragraph 2 of Article II, the number and type of fishing vessel involved and the geographical areas in which such fishing vessels operate; and
      (b) any agreement reached under paragraph 3 of Article II.

8.   (a) Each Party shall report promptly to FAO all relevant information regarding any activities of fishing vessels flying its flag that undermine the effectiveness of international conservation and management measures, including the identity of the fishing vessel or vessels involved and measures imposed by the Party in respect of such activities. Reports on measures imposed by a Party may be subject to such limitations as may be required by national legislation with respect to confidentiality, including, in particular, confidentiality regarding measures that are not yet final.

      (b) Each Party, where it has reasonable grounds to believe that a fishing vessel not entitled to fly its flag has engaged in any activity that undermines the effectiveness of international conservation and management measures, shall draw this to the attention of the flag State concerned and may, as appropriate, draw it to the attention of FAO. It shall provide the flag State with full supporting evidence and may provide FAO with a summary of such evidence. FAO shall not circulate such information until such time as the flag State has had an opportunity to comment on the allegation and evidence submitted, or to object as the case may be.

9.   Each Party shall inform FAO of any cases where the Party, pursuant to paragraph 5 (d) of Article III, has granted an authorization notwithstanding the provisions of paragraph 5 (a) or 5 (b) of Article III. The information shall include pertinent data permitting the identification of the fishing vessel and the owner or operator and, as appropriate, any other information relevant to the Party's decision.

10.   FAO shall circulate promptly the information provided under paragraphs 5, 6, 7, 8 and 9 of this Article to all Parties, and, on request, individually to any Party. FAO shall also, subject to any restrictions imposed by the Party concerned regarding the distribution of information, provide such information promptly on request individually to any global, regional or subregional fisheries organization.

11.   The Parties shall exchange information relating to the implementation of this Agreement, including through FAO and other appropriate global, regional and subregional fisheries organizations.

Article VII
Cooperation with Developing Countries

      The Parties shall cooperate, at a global, regional, subregional or bilateral level, and, as appropriate, with the support of FAO and other international or regional organizations, to provide assistance, including technical assistance, to Parties that are developing countries in order to assist them in fulfilling their obligations under this Agreement.

Article VIII
Non-Parties

1.   The Parties shall encourage any State not party to this Agreement to accept this Agreement and shall encourage any non-Party to adopt laws and regulations consistent with the provisions of this Agreement.

2.   The Parties shall cooperate in a manner consistent with this Agreement and with international law to the end that fishing vessels entitled to fly the flags of non-Parties do not engage in activities that undermine the effectiveness of international conservation and management measures.

3.   The Parties shall exchange information amongst themselves, either directly or through FAO, with respect to activities of fishing vessels flying the flags of non-Parties that undermine the effectiveness of international conservation and management measures.

Article IX
Settlement of Disputes

1.   Any Party may seek consultations with any other Party or Parties on any dispute with regard to the interpretation or application of the provisions of this Agreement with a view to reaching a mutually satisfactory solution as soon as possible.

2.   In the event that the dispute is not resolved through these consultations within a reasonable period of time, the Parties in question shall consult among themselves as soon as possible with a view to having the dispute settled by negotiation, inquiry, mediation, conciliation, arbitration, judicial settlement or other peaceful means of their own choice.

3.   Any dispute of this character not so resolved shall, with the consent of all Parties to the dispute, be referred for settlement to the International Court of Justice, to the International Tribunal for the Law of the Sea upon entry into force of the 1982 United Nations Convention on the Law of the Sea or to arbitration. In the case of failure to reach agreement on referral to the International Court of Justice, to the International Tribunal for the Law of the Sea or to arbitration, the Parties shall continue to consult and cooperate with a view to reaching settlement of the dispute in accordance with the rules of international law relating to the conservation of living marine resources.

Article X
Acceptance

1.   This Agreement shall be open to acceptance by any Member or Associate Member of FAO, and to any non-member State that is a member of the United Nations, or of any of the specialized agencies of the United Nations or of the International Atomic Energy Agency.

2.   Acceptance of this Agreement shall be effected by the deposit of an instrument of acceptance with the Director-General of FAO, hereinafter referred to as the Director-General.

3.   The Director-General shall inform all Parties, all Members and Associate Members of FAO and the Secretary-General of the United Nations of all instruments of acceptance received.

4.   When a regional economic integration organization becomes a Party to this Agreement, such regional economic integration organization shall, in accordance with the provisions of Article II.7 of the FAO Constitution, as

appropriate, notify such modifications or clarifications to its declaration of competence submitted under Article II.5 of the FAO Constitution as may be necessary in light of its acceptance of this Agreement. Any Party to this Agreement may, at any time, request a regional economic integration organization that is a Party to this Agreement to provide information as to which, as between the regional economic integration organization and its Member States, is responsible for the implementation of any particular matter covered by this Agreement. The regional economic integration organization shall provide this information within a reasonable time.

Article XI
Entry into Force

1.   This Agreement shall enter into force as from the date of receipt by the Director-General of the twenty-fifth instrument of acceptance.
2.   For the purpose of this Article, an instrument deposited by a regional economic integration organization shall not be counted as additional to those deposited by member States of such an organization.

Article XII
Reservations

Acceptance of this Agreement may be made subject to reservations which shall become effective only upon unanimous acceptance by all Parties to this Agreement. The Director-General shall notify forthwith all Parties of any reservation. Parties not having replied within three months from the date of the notification shall be deemed to have accepted the reservation. Failing such acceptance, the State or regional economic integration organization making the reservation shall not become a Party to this Agreement.

Article XIII
Amendments

1.   Any proposal by a Party for the amendment of this Agreement shall be communicated to the Director-General.
2.   Any proposed amendment of this Agreement received by the Director-General from a Party shall be presented to a regular or special session of the Conference for approval and, if the amendment involves important technical changes or imposes additional obligations on the Parties, it shall be considered by an advisory committee of specialists convened by FAO prior to the Conference.
3.   Notice of any proposed amendment of this Agreement shall be transmitted to the Parties by the Director-General not later than the time when the agenda of the session of the Conference at which the matter is to be considered is dispatched.
4.   Any such proposed amendment of this Agreement shall require the approval of the Conference and shall come into force as from the thirtieth day after acceptance by two-thirds of the Parties. Amendments involving new obligations for Parties, however, shall come into force in respect of each Party only on acceptance by it and as from the thirtieth day after such acceptance. Any amendment shall be deemed to involve new obligations for Parties unless the Conference, in approving the amendment, decides otherwise by consensus.
5.   The instruments of acceptance of amendments involving new obligations shall be deposited with the Director-General, who shall inform all Parties of the receipt of acceptance and the entry into force of amendments.

6.   For the purpose of this Article, an instrument deposited by a regional economic integration organization shall not be counted as additional to those deposited by member States of such an organization.

Article XIV
Withdrawal

Any Party may withdraw from this Agreement at any time after the expiry of two years from the date upon which the Agreement entered into force with respect to that Party, by giving written notice of such withdrawal to the Director-General who shall immediately inform all the Parties and the Members and Associate Members of FAO of such withdrawal. Withdrawal shall become effective at the end of the calendar year following that in which the notice of withdrawal has been received by the Director-General.

Article XV
Duties of the Depositary

The Director-General shall be the Depositary of this Agreement. The Depositary shall:
  (a) send certified copies of this Agreement to each Member and Associate Member of FAO and to such non-member States as may become party to this Agreement;
  (b) arrange for the registration of this Agreement, upon its entry into force, with the Secretariat of the United Nations in accordance with Article 102 of the Charter of the United Nations;
  (c) inform each Member and Associate Member of FAO and any non-member States as may become Party to this Agreement of:
      (i)   instruments of acceptance deposited in accordance with Article X;
      (ii)   the date of entry into force of this Agreement in accordance with Article XI;
      (iii) proposals for and the entry into force of amendments to this Agreement in accordance with Article XIII;
      (iv)   withdrawals from this Agreement pursuant to Article XIV.

Article XVI
Authentic Texts

The Arabic, Chinese, English, French, and Spanish texts of this Agreement are equally authentic.

III. Code of Conduct for Responsible Fisheries

Background

1.   Pursuant to the recommendations of the Committee on Fisheries at its nineteenth and twentieth sessions, and the instructions of the Council at its one hundred and second, one hundred and third, one hundred and fourth and one hundred and seventh sessions and the Conference at its twenty-seventh session, the FAO Secretariat undertook the preparation of a draft Code of Conduct for Responsible Fisheries which, after consideration by the Committee on Fisheries at its 21st session, was presented to the Council at its one hundred and eighth session with a view to taking the necessary measures to ensure the finalization of the Code in order to submit the final text to the Conference at its twenty-eighth session in October 1995. To that end, the Council established an open-ended Technical Committee, which held its first session in parallel with the Council from 5 to 9 June 1995, with the possibility of holding one or two additional sessions prior to its next session in October 1995.

2.   According to the instructions of the FAO governing bodies, the draft Code was formulated to be consistent with the 1982 United Nations Convention on the Law of the Sea, taking into account the 1992 Declaration of Cancún, the 1992 Rio Declaration and the provisions of Agenda 21 of the United Nations Conference on Environment and Development (UNCED), the conclusions and recommendations of the 1992 FAO Technical Consultation on High Seas Fishing, the Strategy endorsed by the 1984 FAO World Conference on Fisheries Management and Development, and other relevant instruments. It also took into account the outcome of the United Nations Conference on Straddling Fish Stocks and Highly Migratory Fish Stocks.

3.   The Draft Code of Conduct consisted of five introductory articles: Nature and scope; Objectives; Relationship with other international instruments; Implementation, monitoring and updating; and Application of the Code to developing countries. These introductory articles were followed by an article on General principles which preceded the six thematic articles on: Fisheries management; Fishing operations; Aquaculture development; Integration of fisheries into coastal area management; Post-harvest practices and trade; and Fisheries research. The Agreement to Promote Compliance with International Conservation and Management Measures by Fishing Vessels on the High Seas forms an integral part of the Code. In addition, and in support of the implementation of the Code, technical guidelines were elaborated by the FAO Secretariat.

4.   The Conference at its twenty-seventh session recommended that the General Principles of the Code be prepared on a "fast track" and accordingly, as a first step, a draft text of the General Principles was reviewed by an informal working group of government-nominated experts, which met in Rome from 21 to 25 February 1994. Participation in the Working Group of Experts from developing countries was made possible by an ad hoc contribution of the European Commission (which covered their travel costs). The Working Group provided guidance for the formulation of a new Secretariat draft of the General Principles. The new draft was widely circulated to all FAO members and Associate Members as well as intergovernmental and non-governmental organizations. Comments received

on the second version of the General Principles were incorporated together with proposals for an alternative text. The document was also the subject of informal consultations with non-governmental organizations on the occasion of the fourth session of the United Nations Conference on Straddling Fish Stocks and Highly Migratory Fish Stocks, held in August 1994 in New York.

5.   In order to facilitate consideration of the full text of the draft Code by FAO Governing Bodies, the Director-General proposed to the Council at its one hundred and sixth session in June 1994 that it organize a technical consultation on the Code of Conduct for Responsible Fishing, open to all FAO members, interested non-members, intergovernmental and non-governmental organizations, in order to provide an opportunity for the widest involvement at an early stage of its elaboration.

6.   The Technical Consultation was held at Rome from 26 September to 5 October 1994. Participation of developing countries in the Technical Consultation was facilitated by the generous response of France, Japan, Mexico, Norway, Spain and the United States of America to FAO's invitation to provide financial support. The Consultation had the opportunity to review thoroughly all the articles of the complete Draft Code of Conduct. An alternative Secretariat draft was then prepared on the basis of comments made during the discussions in plenary and specific drafting changes were submitted in writing during the Consultation. The Consultation was also able to review in detail the alternative draft of three of the six thematic articles of the Code, i.e., article 6 (Fisheries management), article 7 (Fishing operations)(except principles marked with an asterisk) and article 9 (Integration of fisheries into coastal area management). As agreed, the Secretariat prepared a short administrative report which was presented as an information paper to the Committee on Fisheries (COFI).

7.   The Secretariat, recognizing that a number of paragraphs of the Draft Code would probably be affected by the outcome of the United Nations Conference on Straddling Fish Stocks and Highly Migratory Fish Stocks, proposed to the Technical Consultation and to the Council at its one hundred and seventh session (Rome, 15-24 November 1994) that the final wording of those principles dealing mainly with high-seas issues, which indeed formed only a small part of the Code, should be left in abeyance pending the outcome of the United Nations Conference which had planned for two more sessions in 1995. The Council generally endorsed the proposed procedure, noting that, following decisions by COFI, the Code would be submitted in June 1995 to the FAO Council, which would then decide upon the necessity for a technical committee to meet parallel to that session of the Council in order to elaborate further the detailed provisions of the Code if required.

8.   Based upon the substantial comments and detailed suggestions received at the Technical Consultation, the Secretariat elaborated a revised draft of the Code of Conduct for Responsible Fisheries. However, it was noted that comments received were in some cases accommodated in different sections of the Code, wherever they fitted best. The revised draft of the Code was submitted to the Committee on Fisheries at its twenty-first session, held from 10 to 15 March 1995.

9.   The principles dealing mainly with issues being analysed at the United Nations Conference were concentrated in article 6 (Fisheries management) and article 7 (Fishing operations) and were marked with an

asterisk. However, it was noted that some of those asterisked principles dealt not only with high seas but also with inland waters and exclusive economic zones. Written comments on those paragraphs received by the Secretariat were also presented in an information document to COFI.

10.   The Committee on Fisheries was also informed that the United Nations Conference was expected to conclude its work in August 1995. The relevant part of the draft text of the Code could then be reconciled with the language agreed upon at the United Nations Conference in accordance with a mechanism decided by the Committee and the Council, before submission of the complete Code for adoption at the twenty-eighth session of the FAO Conference, in October 1995.

11.   The Committee was informed of the progress achieved in the elaboration of the Code of Conduct for Responsible Fisheries. It was also informed of the various steps the Secretariat had undertaken for the preparation of the draft Code of Conduct for consideration by the Committee on Fisheries and its further submission to the Council with a view to submitting the final text to the twenty-eighth session of the Conference in October 1995. The Committee stressed the importance of the Code of Conduct for Responsible Fisheries as an instrument which could support the implementation of the 1982 United Nations Convention on the Law of the Sea and UNCED. The Committee established an open-ended Working Group to review the draft text of the Code. The Working Group met from 10 to 14 March 1995.

12.   Following directives from COFI, the open-ended Working Group undertook a detailed revision of the draft Code in continuation of the work carried out by the Technical Consultation. It completed and approved the text of article 8 (Aquaculture development), article 10 (Post-harvest practices and trade) and article 11 (Fisheries research). In view of the time constraints, the Working Group then decided to provide directives to the Secretariat to redraft articles 1 to 4bis. However, some of the directives went beyond consideration of those articles and touched on the character of the draft Code as a whole, and it would have been difficult to incorporate them without the benefit of wider discussion. Accordingly, at that stage, only those changes which could be readily incorporated were inserted into the revised text. The Group also recommended that the text in its entirety should maintain a balance to reflect the objectives and purposes of responsible fisheries. It was further recommended that the elements of research and cooperation as well as aquaculture should be included in article 5 (General principles) to reflect issues developed in the Thematic Articles of the Code.

13.   Finally, the open-ended Working Group recommended additional consultations to finalize the analyses of the text in terms of its form and content. Accordingly, the Group supported the Council proposal to set up open-ended technical committees for that purpose. The Group also recommended that once agreement was reached on the substance, it would be convenient to harmonize legal, technical and idiomatic aspects of the Code, in order to facilitate its final approval.

14.   The Committee agreed to the proposal endorsed by the Council at its one hundred and seventh session on the mechanism to finalize the Code, i.e., that the final wording of those principles dealing mainly with issues concerning straddling fish stocks and highly migratory fish stocks, which formed only a small part of the Code, should be re-examined in the light of

the outcome of the United Nations Conference. However, some delegations
expressed concern that the Code should not be delayed since it covered not
only straddling fish stocks and highly migratory fish stocks, but all fishery
management matters.

15.   The Committee took note of the progress achieved in the review of
the draft Code of Conduct for Responsible Fisheries by the open-ended
Working Group and urged that the entire Code be completed in time for
adoption by the FAO Conference at its twenty-eighth session in October
1995.

16.   The report of the open-ended Working Group was presented to the
Ministerial Meeting on Fisheries held on 14 and 15 March 1995. The Rome
Consensus on World Fisheries emanating from the meeting urged that
"Governments and international organizations take prompt action to complete
the International Code of Conduct for Responsible Fisheries with a view to
submitting the final text to the FAO Conference in October 1995".

17.   The Council was presented with a revised version of the Code of
Conduct. As indicated above, articles 8 to 11 had already been finalized;
articles 6 and 7 had been revised twice by the Technical Consultation, but
asterisked principles remained in abeyance pending the outcome of the
United Nations Conference; the Secretariat had revised articles 1 to 4bis
following directives by COFI; article 5 (General principles), which had been
extensively considered on an earlier occasion, remained unchanged except
for the inclusion of one principle on aquaculture and another on the
promotion of cooperation and research, as requested by COFI.

18.   The Council established an open-ended Technical Committee which
held its first session from 5 to 9 June 1995 and was attended by 29 FAO
member countries and one observer, with a broad regional representation.
A number of relevant intergovernmental and non-governmental organizations
also participated.

19.   The Council was informed by the Technical Committee that it had
undertaken a thorough review of articles 1 to 5, including the Introduction.
It had also examined, enhanced and approved articles 8 to 11, which had
already been revised previously, and endorsed all of them. The Council was
also informed that the Committee had started the revision of article 6, with
the exclusion of the provisions marked with an asterisk. Therefore, articles
6 and 7 remained to be finalized.

20.   In the light of progress achieved, the Council commended and
approved the work carried out by the Technical Committee and endorsed its
recommendation for a second session to be held from 25 to 29 September
1995 to complete the revision of the Code once the Secretariat had
harmonized the texts linguistically and juridically, and taking into account
the outcome of the United Nations Conference on Straddling Fish Stocks and
Highly Migratory Fish Stocks. If necessary, a third session would be held
prior to the session of the Council in October 1995.

21.   A revised version of the Code, as approved by the Open-Ended
Technical Committee at its first session (5-9 June 1995) and endorsed by the
Council at its one hundred and eighth session, was issued, both as a
Conference document (C 95/20) and as a working paper for the second
session of the Technical Committee (document WP/1). Elements pending

agreement were shown in shadow, for example, in articles 3, 5 and 6. In order to facilitate analysis reference to the original enumeration had been retained, while additions had been referred to as "*bis*", "*ter*", etc.

22.   In order to facilitate the finalization of the entire Code, the Secretariat proceeded to prepare document WP/1 (Addendum) entitled "Secretariat proposals for article 6, Fisheries management, and article 7, Fishing operations, of the Code of Conduct for Responsible Fisheries", taking into account the Agreement for the Implementation of the Provisions of the United Nations Convention on the Law of the Sea of 10 December 1982 relating to the Conservation and Management of Straddling Fish Stocks and Highly Migratory Fish Stocks, adopted by the United Nations Conference in August 1995.

23.   The Secretariat also completed proposals for the harmonization of the text on legal and linguistic aspects and made available to the Committee in three languages for the session (English, French and Spanish). At the opening of the second session of the Technical Committee, the Secretariat requested that, on the basis of the Conference document (C 95/20), which had also been issued in Arabic and Chinese, concerned delegations should provide the Secretariat with written comments to be taken into account when issuing the revised version.

24.   The Open-ended Technical Committee met from 25 to 29 September 1995, with a wide representation of regions and interested organizations, and worked in a full spirit of collaboration and successfully concluded its mandate, finalizing and endorsing all articles and the Code as a whole. The Technical Committee agreed that the negotiations of the text of the Code had been finalized. It requested the Secretariat to proceed with the final editing of the text according to agreements reached during the closing session in various recommendations for linguistic harmonization. It instructed the Secretariat to submit the new version as document C 95/20 (Rev.1) to the Council at its one hundred and ninth session and to the Conference at its twenty-eighth session for adoption. The Secretariat was also requested to prepare for the Conference the required draft resolution, which should include a call on countries to ratify as a matter of urgency the Compliance Agreement adopted at the last session of the Conference.

25.   With regard to linguistic harmonization, the Open-Ended Informal Group on Language Harmonization held an additional session and, together with the Secretariat, completed the harmonization on the basis of the text as adopted at the closing plenary session.

Code of Conduct for Responsible Fisheries

INTRODUCTION

Fisheries, including aquaculture, provide a vital source of food, employment, recreation, trade and economic well being for people throughout the world, both for present and future generations and should therefore be conducted in a responsible manner. This Code sets out principles and international standards of behaviour for responsible practices with a view to ensuring the effective conservation, management and development of living aquatic resources, with due respect for the ecosystem and biodiversity. The Code recognises the nutritional, economic, social, environmental and cultural importance of fisheries, and the interests of all those concerned with the fishery sector. The Code takes into account the biological characteristics of the resources and their environment and the interests of consumers and other users. States and all those involved in fisheries are encouraged to apply the Code and give effect to it.

ARTICLE 1 - NATURE AND SCOPE OF THE CODE

1.1   This Code is voluntary. However, certain parts of it are based on relevant rules of international law, including those reflected in the United Nations Convention on the Law of the Sea of 10 December 1982. The Code also contains provisions that may be or have already been given binding effect by means of other obligatory legal instruments amongst the Parties, such as the Agreement to Promote Compliance with International Conservation and Management Measures by Fishing Vessels on the High Seas, 1993, which, according to FAO Conference resolution 15/93, paragraph 3, forms an integral part of the Code.
1.2   The Code is global in scope, and is directed toward members and non-members of FAO, fishing entities, subregional, regional and global organizations, whether governmental or non-governmental, and all persons concerned with the conservation of fishery resources and management and development of fisheries, such as fishers, those engaged in processing and marketing of fish and fishery products and other users of the aquatic environment in relation to fisheries.
1.3   The Code provides principles and standards applicable to the conservation, management and development of all fisheries. It also covers the capture, processing and trade of fish and fishery products, fishing operations, aquaculture, fisheries research and the integration of fisheries into coastal area management.
1.4   In this Code, the reference to States includes the European Community in matters within its competence, and the term fisheries applies equally to capture fisheries and aquaculture.

ARTICLE 2 - OBJECTIVES OF THE CODE

The objectives of the Code are to:
(a)   establish principles, in accordance with the relevant rules of international law, for responsible fishing and fisheries activities, taking into account all their relevant biological, technological, economic, social, environmental and commercial aspects;
(b)   establish principles and criteria for the elaboration and implementation of national policies for responsible

conservation of fisheries resources and fisheries management and development;

(c)   serve as an instrument of reference to help States to establish or to improve the legal and institutional framework required for the exercise of responsible fisheries and in the formulation and implementation of appropriate measures;

(d)   provide guidance which may be used where appropriate in the formulation and implementation of international agreements and other legal instruments, both binding and voluntary;

(e)   facilitate and promote technical, financial and other cooperation in conservation of fisheries resources and fisheries management and development;

(f)   promote the contribution of fisheries to food security and food quality, giving priority to the nutritional needs of local communities;

(g)   promote protection of living aquatic resources and their environments and coastal areas;

(h)   promote the trade of fish and fishery products in conformity with relevant international rules and avoid the use of measures that constitute hidden barriers to such trade;

(i)   promote research on fisheries as well as on associated ecosystems and relevant environmental factors; and

(j)   provide standards of conduct for all persons involved in the fisheries sector.

ARTICLE 3 - RELATIONSHIP WITH OTHER INTERNATIONAL INSTRUMENTS

3.1   The Code is to be interpreted and applied in conformity with the relevant rules of international law, as reflected in the United Nations Convention on the Law of the Sea, 1982. Nothing in this Code prejudices the rights, jurisdiction and duties of States under international law as reflected in the Convention.

3.2   The Code is also to be interpreted and applied:

(a)   in a manner consistent with the relevant provisions of the Agreement for the Implementation of the Provisions of the United Nations Convention on the Law of the Sea of 10 December 1982 Relating to the Conservation and Management of Straddling Fish Stocks and Highly Migratory Fish Stocks;

(b)   in accordance with other applicable rules of international law, including the respective obligations of States pursuant to international agreements to which they are party; and

(c)   in the light of the 1992 Declaration of Cancún, the 1992 Rio Declaration on Environment and Development, and Agenda 21 adopted by the United Nations Conference on Environment and Development (UNCED), in particular Chapter 17 of Agenda 21, and other relevant declarations and international instruments.

ARTICLE 4 - IMPLEMENTATION, MONITORING AND UPDATING

4.1   All members and non-members of FAO, fishing entities and relevant subregional, regional and global organizations, whether governmental or non-governmental, and all persons concerned with the conservation, management and utilization of fisheries resources and trade in fish and fishery products should collaborate in the fulfilment and implementation of the objectives and principles contained in this Code.

4.2   FAO, in accordance with its role within the United Nations system, will monitor the application and implementation of the Code and its effects on fisheries and the Secretariat will report accordingly to the Committee on Fisheries (COFI). All States, whether members or non-members of FAO, as well as relevant international organizations, whether governmental or non-governmental should actively cooperate with FAO in this work.

4.3   FAO, through its competent bodies, may revise the Code, taking into account developments in fisheries as well as reports to COFI on the implementation of the Code.

4.4   States and international organizations, whether governmental or non-governmental, should promote the understanding of the Code among those involved in fisheries, including, where practicable, by the introduction of schemes which would promote voluntary acceptance of the Code and its effective application.

ARTICLE 5 - SPECIAL REQUIREMENTS OF DEVELOPING COUNTRIES

5.1   The capacity of developing countries to implement the recommendations of this Code should be duly taken into account.

5.2   In order to achieve the objectives of this Code and to support its effective implementation, countries, relevant intergovernmental and non-governmental organizations and financial institutions should give full recognition to the special circumstances and requirements of developing countries, including in particular the least-developed among them, and small island developing countries. States, relevant intergovernmental and non-governmental organizations and financial institutions should work for the adoption of measures to address the needs of developing countries, especially in the areas of financial and technical assistance, technology transfer, training and scientific cooperation and in enhancing their ability to develop their own fisheries as well as to participate in high seas fisheries, including access to such fisheries.

ARTICLE 6 - GENERAL PRINCIPLES

6.1   States and users of living aquatic resources should conserve aquatic ecosystems. The right to fish carries with it the obligation to do so in a responsible manner so as to ensure effective conservation and management of the living aquatic resources.

6.2   Fisheries management should promote the maintenance of the quality, diversity and availability of fishery resources in sufficient quantities for present and future generations in the context of food security, poverty alleviation and sustainable development. Management measures should not only ensure the conservation of target species but also of species belonging to the same ecosystem or associated with or dependent upon the target species.

6.3   States should prevent overfishing and excess fishing capacity and should implement management measures to ensure that fishing effort is commensurate with the productive capacity of the fishery resources and their sustainable utilization. States should take measures to rehabilitate populations as far as possible and when appropriate.

6.4   Conservation and management decisions for fisheries should be based on the best scientific evidence available, also taking into account traditional knowledge of the resources and their habitat, as well as relevant environmental, economic and social factors. States should assign priority to undertake research and data collection in order to improve scientific and technical knowledge of fisheries including their interaction with the ecosystem. In recognizing the transboundary nature of many aquatic ecosystems, States should encourage bilateral and multilateral cooperation in research, as appropriate.

6.5   States and subregional and regional fisheries management organizations should apply a precautionary approach widely to conservation, management and exploitation of living aquatic resources in order to protect them and preserve the aquatic environment, taking account of the best scientific evidence available. The absence of adequate scientific information should not be used as a reason for postponing or failing to take measures to conserve target species, associated or dependent species and non-target species and their environment.

6.6   Selective and environmentally safe fishing gear and practices should be further developed and applied, to the extent practicable, in order to maintain biodiversity and to conserve the population structure and aquatic ecosystems and protect fish quality. Where proper selective and environmentally safe fishing gear and practices exist, they should be . recognized and accorded a priority in establishing conservation and management measures for fisheries. States and users of aquatic ecosystems should minimize waste, catch of non-target species, both fish and non-fish species, and impacts on associated or dependent species.

6.7   The harvesting, handling, processing and distribution of fish and fishery products should be carried out in a manner which will maintain the nutritional value, quality and safety of the products, reduce waste and minimize negative impacts on the environment.

6.8   All critical fisheries habitats in marine and fresh water ecosystems, such as wetlands, mangroves, reefs, lagoons, nursery and spawning, should be protected and rehabilitated as far as possible and where necessary. Particular effort should be made to protect such habitats from destruction, degradation, pollution and other significant impacts resulting from human activities that threaten the health and viability of the fishery resources.

6.9   States should ensure that their fisheries interests, including the need for conservation of the resources, are taken into account in the multiple uses of the coastal zone and are integrated into coastal area management, planning and development.

6.10   Within their respective competences and in accordance with international law, including within the framework of subregional or regional fisheries conservation and management organizations or arrangements, States should ensure compliance with and enforcement of conservation and management measures and establish effective mechanisms, as appropriate, to monitor and control the activities of fishing vessels and fishing support vessels.

6.11   States authorizing fishing and fishing support vessels to fly their flags should exercise effective control over those vessels so as to ensure the proper application of this Code. They should ensure that the activities of such vessels do not undermine the effectiveness of conservation and management measures taken in accordance with international law and adopted at the national, subregional, regional or global levels. States should also ensure that vessels flying their flags fulfil their obligations concerning the collection and provision of data relating to their fishing activities.

6.12   States should, within their respective competences and in accordance with international law, cooperate at subregional, regional and global levels through fisheries management organizations, other international agreements or other arrangements to promote conservation and management, ensure responsible fishing and ensure effective conservation and protection of living aquatic resources throughout their range of distribution, taking into account the need for compatible measures in areas within and beyond national jurisdiction.

6.13   States should, to the extent permitted by national laws and regulations, ensure that decision making processes are transparent and achieve timely solutions to urgent matters. States, in accordance with appropriate procedures, should facilitate consultation and the effective participation of industry, fishworkers, environmental and other interested organizations in decision making with respect to the development of laws and policies related to fisheries management, development, international lending and aid.

6.14   International trade in fish and fishery products should be conducted in accordance with the principles, rights and obligations established in the World Trade Organization (WTO) Agreement and other relevant international agreements. States should ensure that their policies, programmes and practices related to trade in fish and fishery products do not result in obstacles to this trade, environmental degradation or negative social, including nutritional, impacts.

6.15   States should cooperate in order to prevent disputes. All disputes relating to fishing activities and practices should be resolved in a timely, peaceful and cooperative manner, in accordance with applicable international agreements or as may otherwise be agreed between the parties. Pending settlement of a dispute, the States concerned should make every effort to enter into provisional arrangements of a practical nature which should be without prejudice to the final outcome of any dispute settlement procedure.

6.16   States, recognising the paramount importance to fishers and fishfarmers of understanding the conservation and management of the fishery resources on which they depend, should promote awareness of responsible fisheries through education and training. They should ensure that fishers and fishfarmers are involved in the policy formulation and implementation process, also with a view to facilitating the implementation of the Code.

6.17   States should ensure that fishing facilities and equipment as well as all fisheries activities allow for safe, healthy and fair working and living conditions and meet internationally agreed standards adopted by relevant international organizations.

6.18   Recognizing the important contributions of artisanal and small-scale fisheries to employment, income and food security, States should appropriately protect the rights of fishers and fishworkers, particularly those engaged in subsistence, small-scale and artisanal fisheries, to a secure and just livelihood, as well as preferential access, where appropriate, to traditional fishing grounds and resources in the waters under their national jurisdiction.

6.19   States should consider aquaculture, including culture-based fisheries, as a means to promote diversification of income and diet. In so doing, States should ensure that resources are used responsibly and adverse impacts on the environment and on local communities are minimized.

ARTICLE 7 - FISHERIES MANAGEMENT

7.1   General

7.1.1   States and all those engaged in fisheries management should, through an appropriate policy, legal and institutional framework, adopt measures for the long-term conservation and sustainable use of fisheries resources. Conservation and management measures, whether at local, national, subregional or regional levels, should be based on the best scientific evidence available and be designed to ensure the long-term sustainability of fishery resources at levels which promote the objective of their optimum utilization and maintain their availability for present and future generations; short term considerations should not compromise these objectives.

7.1.2   Within areas under national jurisdiction, States should seek to identify relevant domestic parties having a legitimate interest in the use and management of fisheries resources and establish arrangements for consulting them to gain their collaboration in achieving responsible fisheries.

7.1.3   For transboundary fish stocks, straddling fish stocks, highly migratory fish stocks and high seas fish stocks, where these are exploited by two or more States, the States concerned, including the relevant coastal States in the case of straddling and highly migratory stocks, should cooperate to ensure effective conservation and management of the resources. This should be achieved, where appropriate, through the establishment of a bilateral, subregional or regional fisheries organization or arrangement.

7.1.4   A subregional or regional fisheries management organization or arrangement should include representatives of States in whose jurisdictions the resources occur, as well as representatives from States which have a real interest in the fisheries on the resources outside national jurisdictions. Where a subregional or regional fisheries management organization or arrangement exists and has the competence to establish conservation and management measures, those States should cooperate by becoming a member of such organization or a participant in such arrangement, and actively participate in its work.

7.1.5   A State which is not a member of a subregional or regional fisheries management organization or is not a participant in a subregional or regional fisheries management arrangement should nevertheless cooperate, in accordance with relevant international agreements and international law, in the conservation and management of the relevant fisheries resources by giving effect to any conservation and management measures adopted by such organization or arrangement.

7.1.6   Representatives from relevant organizations, both governmental and non-governmental, concerned with fisheries should be afforded the opportunity to take part in meetings of subregional and regional fisheries management organizations and arrangements as observers or otherwise, as appropriate, in accordance with the procedures of the organization or arrangement concerned. Such representatives should be given timely access to the records and reports of such meetings, subject to the procedural rules on access to them.

7.1.7   States should establish, within their respective competences and capacities, effective mechanisms for fisheries monitoring, surveillance, control and enforcement to ensure compliance with their conservation and management measures, as well as those adopted by subregional or regional organizations or arrangements.

7.1.8   States should take measures to prevent or eliminate excess fishing capacity and should ensure that levels of fishing effort are commensurate with the sustainable use of fishery resources as a means of ensuring the effectiveness of conservation and management measures.

7.1.9   States and subregional or regional fisheries management organizations and arrangements should ensure transparency in the mechanisms for fisheries management and in the related decision-making process.

7.1.10 States and subregional or regional fisheries management organizations and arrangements should give due publicity to conservation and management measures and ensure that laws, regulations and other legal rules governing their implementation are effectively disseminated. The bases and purposes of such measures should be explained to users of the resource in order to facilitate their application and thus gain increased support in the implementation of such measures.

7.2   Management objectives

7.2.1   Recognizing that long-term sustainable use of fisheries resources is the overriding objective of conservation and management, States and subregional or regional fisheries management organizations and arrangements should, inter alia, adopt appropriate measures, based on the best scientific evidence available, which are designed to maintain or restore stocks at levels capable of producing maximum sustainable yield, as qualified by relevant environmental and economic factors, including the special requirements of developing countries.

7.2.2   Such measures should provide inter alia that:
(a)   excess fishing capacity is avoided and exploitation of the stocks remains economically viable;
(b)   the economic conditions under which fishing industries operate promote responsible fisheries;
(c)   the interests of fishers, including those engaged in subsistence, small-scale and artisanal fisheries, are taken into account;
(d)   biodiversity of aquatic habitats and ecosystems is conserved and endangered species are protected;
(e)   depleted stocks are allowed to recover or, where appropriate, are actively restored;
(f)   adverse environmental impacts on the resources from human activities are assessed and, where appropriate, corrected; and
(g)   pollution, waste, discards, catch by lost or abandoned gear, catch of non-target species, both fish and non- fish species, and impacts on associated or dependent species are minimized, through measures including, to the extent practicable, the development and use of selective, environmentally safe and cost-effective fishing gear and techniques.

7.2.3   States should assess the impacts of environmental factors on target stocks and species belonging to the same ecosystem or associated with or dependent upon the target stocks, and assess the relationship among the populations in the ecosystem.

7.3   Management framework and procedures

7.3.1   To be effective, fisheries management should be concerned with the whole stock unit over its entire area of distribution and take into account previously agreed management measures established and applied in the same region, all removals and the biological unity and other biological characteristics of the stock. The best scientific evidence available should be used to determine, inter alia, the area of distribution of the resource and the area through which it migrates during its life cycle.

7.3.2   In order to conserve and manage transboundary fish stocks, straddling fish stocks, highly migratory fish stocks and high seas fish stocks throughout their range, conservation and management measures established for such stocks in accordance with the respective competences of relevant States or, where appropriate, through subregional and regional fisheries management organizations and arrangements, should be compatible.

Compatibility should be achieved in a manner consistent with the rights, competences and interests of the States concerned.
7.3.3   Long-term management objectives should be translated into management actions, formulated as a fishery management plan or other management framework.
7.3.4   States and, where appropriate, subregional or regional fisheries management organizations and arrangements should foster and promote international cooperation and coordination in all matters related to fisheries, including information gathering and exchange, fisheries research, management and development.
7.3.5   States seeking to take any action through a non-fishery organization which may affect the conservation and management measures taken by a competent subregional or regional fisheries management organization or arrangement should consult with the latter, in advance to the extent practicable, and take its views into account.

7.4   *Data gathering and management advice*

7.4.1   When considering the adoption of conservation and management measures, the best scientific evidence available should be taken into account in order to evaluate the current state of the fishery resources and the possible impact of the proposed measures on the resources.
7.4.2   Research in support of fishery conservation and management should be promoted, including research on the resources and on the effects of climatic, environmental and socio-economic factors. The results of such research should be disseminated to interested parties.
7.4.3   Studies should be promoted which provide an understanding of the costs, benefits and effects of alternative management options designed to rationalize fishing, in particular, options relating to excess fishing capacity and excessive levels of fishing effort.
7.4.4   States should ensure that timely, complete and reliable statistics on catch and fishing effort are collected and maintained in accordance with applicable international standards and practices and in sufficient detail to allow sound statistical analysis. Such data should be updated regularly and verified through an appropriate system.   States should compile and disseminate such data in a manner consistent with any applicable confidentiality requirements.
7.4.5   In order to ensure sustainable management of fisheries and to enable social and economic objectives to be achieved, sufficient knowledge of social, economic and institutional factors should be developed through data gathering, analysis and research.
7.4.6   States should compile fishery-related and other supporting scientific data relating to fish stocks covered by subregional or regional fisheries management organizations or arrangements in an internationally agreed format and provide them in a timely manner to the organization or arrangement. In cases of stocks which occur in the jurisdiction of more than one State and for which there is no such organization or arrangement, the States concerned should agree on a mechanism for cooperation to compile and exchange such data.
7.4.7   Subregional or regional fisheries management organizations or arrangements should compile data and make them available, in a manner consistent with any applicable confidentiality requirements, in a timely manner and in an agreed format to all members of these organizations and other interested parties in accordance with agreed procedures.

7.5   Precautionary approach

7.5.1   States should apply the precautionary approach widely to conservation, management and exploitation of living aquatic resources in order to protect them and preserve the aquatic environment. The absence of adequate scientific information should not be used as a reason for postponing or failing to take conservation and management measures.
7.5.2   In implementing the precautionary approach, States should take into account, inter alia, uncertainties relating to the size and productivity of the stocks, reference points, stock condition in relation to such reference points, levels and distribution of fishing mortality and the impact of fishing activities, including discards, on non-target and associated or dependent species, as well as environmental and socio-economic conditions.
7.5.3   States and subregional or regional fisheries management organizations and arrangements should, on the basis of the best scientific evidence available, inter alia, determine:
    (a)   stock specific target reference points, and, at the same time, the action to be taken if they are exceeded; and
    (b)   stock-specific limit reference points, and, at the same time, the action to be taken if they are exceeded; when a limit reference point is approached, measures should be taken to ensure that it will not be exceeded.
7.5.4   In the case of new or exploratory fisheries, States should adopt as soon as possible cautious conservation and management measures, including, inter alia, catch limits and effort limits. Such measures should remain in force until there are sufficient data to allow assessment of the impact of the fisheries on the long-term sustainability of the stocks, whereupon conservation and management measures based on that assessment should be implemented. The latter measures should, if appropriate, allow for the gradual development of the fisheries.
7.5.5   If a natural phenomenon has a significant adverse impact on the status of living aquatic resources, States should adopt conservation and management measures on an emergency basis to ensure that fishing activity does not exacerbate such adverse impact. States should also adopt such measures on an emergency basis where fishing activity presents a serious threat to the sustainability of such resources. Measures taken on an emergency basis should be temporary and should be based on the best scientific evidence available.

7.6   Management measures

7.6.1   States should ensure that the level of fishing permitted is commensurate with the state of fisheries resources.
7.6.2   States should adopt measures to ensure that no vessel be allowed to fish unless so authorized, in a manner consistent with international law for the high seas or in conformity with national legislation within areas of national jurisdiction.
7.6.3   Where excess fishing capacity exists, mechanisms should be established to reduce capacity to levels commensurate with the sustainable use of fisheries resources so as to ensure that fishers operate under economic conditions that promote responsible fisheries. Such mechanisms should include monitoring the capacity of fishing fleets.
7.6.4   The performance of all existing fishing gear, methods and practices should be examined and measures taken to ensure that fishing gear, methods and practices which are not consistent with responsible fishing are phased out and replaced with more acceptable alternatives. In this process, particular

attention should be given to the impact of such measures on fishing communities, including their ability to exploit the resource.

7.6.5 States and fisheries management organizations and arrangements should regulate fishing in such a way as to avoid the risk of conflict among fishers using different vessels, gear and fishing methods.

7.6.6 When deciding on the use, conservation and management of fisheries resources, due recognition should be given, as appropriate, in accordance with national laws and regulations, to the traditional practices, needs and interests of indigenous people and local fishing communities which are highly dependent on fishery resources for their livelihood.

7.6.7 In the evaluation of alternative conservation and management measures, their cost-effectiveness and social impact should be considered.

7.6.8 The efficacy of conservation and management measures and their possible interactions should be kept under continuous review. Such measures should, as appropriate, be revised or abolished in the light of new information.

7.6.9 States should take appropriate measures to minimize waste, discards, catch by lost or abandoned gear, catch of non-target species, both fish and non-fish species, and negative impacts on associated or dependent species, in particular endangered species. Where appropriate, such measures may include technical measures related to fish size, mesh size or gear, discards, closed seasons and areas and zones reserved for selected fisheries, particularly artisanal fisheries. Such measures should be applied, where appropriate, to protect juveniles and spawners. States and subregional or regional fisheries management organizations and arrangements should promote, to the extent practicable, the development and use of selective, environmentally safe and cost effective gear and techniques.

7.6.10 States and subregional and regional fisheries management organizations and arrangements, in the framework of their respective competences, should introduce measures for depleted resources and those resources threatened with depletion that facilitate the sustained recovery of such stocks. They should make every effort to ensure that resources and habitats critical to the well-being of such resources which have been adversely affected by fishing or other human activities are restored.

7.7   Implementation

7.7.1 States should ensure that an effective legal and administrative framework at the local and national level, as appropriate, is established for fisheries resource conservation and fisheries management.

7.7.2 States should ensure that laws and regulations provide for sanctions applicable in respect of violations which are adequate in severity to be effective, including sanctions which allow for the refusal, withdrawal or suspension of authorizations to fish in the event of non-compliance with conservation and management measures in force.

7.7.3 States, in conformity with their national laws, should implement effective fisheries monitoring, control, surveillance and law enforcement measures including, where appropriate, observer programmes, inspection schemes and vessel monitoring systems. Such measures should be promoted and, where appropriate, implemented by subregional or regional fisheries management organizations and arrangements in accordance with procedures agreed by such organizations or arrangements.

7.7.4 States and subregional or regional fisheries management organizations and arrangements, as appropriate, should agree on the means by which the activities of such organizations and arrangements will be

financed, bearing in mind, inter alia, the relative benefits derived from the fishery and the differing capacities of countries to provide financial and other contributions. Where appropriate, and when possible, such organizations and arrangements should aim to recover the costs of fisheries conservation, management and research.
7.7.5   States which are members of or participants in subregional or regional fisheries management organizations or arrangements should implement internationally agreed measures adopted in the framework of such organizations or arrangements and consistent with international law to deter the activities of vessels flying the flag of non-members or non-participants which engage in activities which undermine the effectiveness of conservation and management measures established by such organizations or arrangements.

7.8   *Financial institutions*

7.8.1   Without prejudice to relevant international agreements, States should encourage banks and financial institutions not to require, as a condition of a loan or mortgage, fishing vessels or fishing support vessels to be flagged in a jurisdiction other than that of the State of beneficial ownership where such a requirement would have the effect of increasing the likelihood of non-compliance with international conservation and management measures.

ARTICLE 8 - FISHING OPERATIONS

8.1   *Duties of all States*

8.1.1   States should ensure that only fishing operations allowed by them are conducted within waters under their jurisdiction and that these operations are carried out in a responsible manner.
8.1.2   States should maintain a record, updated at regular intervals, on all authorizations to fish issued by them.
8.1.3   States should maintain, in accordance with recognized international standards and practices, statistical data, updated at regular intervals, on all fishing operations allowed by them.
8.1.4   States should, in accordance with international law, within the framework of subregional or regional fisheries management organizations or arrangements, cooperate to establish systems for monitoring, control, surveillance and enforcement of applicable measures with respect to fishing operations and related activities in waters outside their national jurisdiction.
8.1.5   States should ensure that health and safety standards are adopted for everyone employed in fishing operations. Such standards should be not less than the minimum requirements of relevant international agreements on conditions of work and service.
8.1.6   States should make arrangements individually, together with other States or with the appropriate international organization to integrate fishing operations into maritime search and rescue systems.
8.1.7   States should enhance through education and training programmes the education and skills of fishers and, where appropriate, their professional qualifications.   Such programmes should take into account agreed international standards and guidelines.
8.1.8   States should, as appropriate, maintain records of fishers which should, whenever possible, contain information on their service and qualifications, including certificates of competency, in accordance with their national laws.

8.1.9   States should ensure that measures applicable in respect of masters and other officers charged with an offence relating to the operation of fishing vessels should include provisions which may permit, inter alia, refusal, withdrawal or suspension of authorizations to serve as masters or officers of a fishing vessel.

8.1.10   States, with the assistance of relevant international organizations, should endeavour to ensure through education and training that all those engaged in fishing operations be given information on the most important provisions of this Code, as well as provisions of relevant international conventions and applicable environmental and other standards that are essential to ensure responsible fishing operations.

8.2   Flag State duties

8.2.1   Flag States should maintain records of fishing vessels entitled to fly their flag and authorized to be used for fishing and should indicate in such records details of the vessels, their ownership and authorization to fish.

8.2.2   Flag States should ensure that no fishing vessels entitled to fly their flag fish on the high seas or in waters under the jurisdiction of other States unless such vessels have been issued with a Certificate of Registry and have been authorized to fish by the competent authorities. Such vessels should carry on board the Certificate of Registry and their authorization to fish.

8.2.3   Fishing vessels authorized to fish on the high seas or in waters under the jurisdiction of a State other than the flag State, should be marked in accordance with uniform and internationally recognizable vessel marking systems such as the FAO Standard Specifications and Guidelines for Marking and Identification of Fishing Vessels.

8.2.4   Fishing gear should be marked in accordance with national legislation in order that the owner of the gear can be identified. Gear marking requirements should take into account uniform and internationally recognizable gear marking systems.

8.2.5   Flag States should ensure compliance with appropriate safety requirements for fishing vessels and fishers in accordance with international conventions, internationally agreed codes of practice and voluntary guidelines. States should adopt appropriate safety requirements for all small vessels not covered by such international conventions, codes of practice or voluntary guidelines.

8.2.6   States not party to the Agreement to Promote Compliance with International Conservation and Management Measures by Vessels Fishing in the High Seas should be encouraged to accept the Agreement and to adopt laws and regulations consistent with the provisions of the Agreement.

8.2.7   Flag States should take enforcement measures in respect of fishing vessels entitled to fly their flag which have been found by them to have contravened applicable conservation and management measures, including, where appropriate, making the contravention of such measures an offence under national legislation. Sanctions applicable in respect of violations should be adequate in severity to be effective in securing compliance and to discourage violations wherever they occur and should deprive offenders of the benefits accruing from their illegal activities. Such sanctions may, for serious violations, include provisions for the refusal, withdrawal or suspension of the authorization to fish.

8.2.8   Flag States should promote access to insurance coverage by owners and charterers of fishing vessels. Owners or charterers of fishing vessels should carry sufficient insurance cover to protect the crew of such vessels and their interests, to indemnify third parties against loss or damage and to protect their own interests.

8.2.9   Flag States should ensure that crew members are entitled to repatriation, taking account of the principles laid down in the "Repatriation of Seafarers Convention (Revised), 1987, (No.166)".
8.2.10 In the event of an accident to a fishing vessel or persons on board a fishing vessel, the flag State of the fishing vessel concerned should provide details of the accident to the State of any foreign national on board the vessel involved in the accident. Such information should also, where practicable, be communicated to the International Maritime Organization.

8.3   Port State duties

8.3.1   Port States should take, through procedures established in their national legislation, in accordance with international law, including applicable international agreements or arrangements, such measures as are necessary to achieve and to assist other States in achieving the objectives of this Code, and should make known to other States details of regulations and measures they have established for this purpose. When taking such measures a port State should not discriminate in form or in fact against the vessels of any other State.
8.3.2   Port States should provide such assistance to flag States as is appropriate, in accordance with the national laws of the port State and international law, when a fishing vessel is voluntarily in a port or at an offshore terminal of the port State and the flag State of the vessel requests the port State for assistance in respect of non-compliance with subregional, regional or global conservation and management measures or with internationally agreed minimum standards for the prevention of pollution and for safety, health and conditions of work on board fishing vessels.

8.4   Fishing activities

8.4.1   States should ensure that fishing is conducted with due regard to the safety of human life and the International Maritime Organization International Regulations for Preventing Collisions at Sea, as well as International Maritime Organization requirements relating to the organization of marine traffic, protection of the marine environment and the prevention of damage to or loss of fishing gear.
8.4.2   States should prohibit dynamiting, poisoning and other comparable destructive fishing practices.
8.4.3   States should make every effort to ensure that documentation with regard to fishing operations, retained catch of fish and non-fish species and, as regards discards, the information required for stock assessment as decided by relevant management bodies, is collected and forwarded systematically to those bodies. States should, as far as possible, establish programmes, such as observer and inspection schemes, in order to promote compliance with applicable measures.
8.4.4   States should promote the adoption of appropriate technology, taking into account economic conditions, for the best use and care of the retained catch.
8.4.5   States, with relevant groups from industry, should encourage the development and implementation of technologies and operational methods that reduce discards. The use of fishing gear and practices that lead to the discarding of catch should be discouraged and the use of fishing gear and practices that increase survival rates of escaping fish should be promoted.
8.4.6   States should cooperate to develop and apply technologies, materials and operational methods that minimize the loss of fishing gear and the ghost fishing effects of lost or abandoned fishing gear.

8.4.7   States should ensure that assessments of the implications of habitat disturbance are carried out prior to the introduction on a commercial scale of new fishing gear, methods and operations to an area.
8.4.8   Research on the environmental and social impacts of fishing gear and, in particular, on the impact of such gear on biodiversity and coastal fishing communities should be promoted.

8.5   *Fishing gear selectivity*

8.5.1   States should require that fishing gear, methods and practices, to the extent practicable, are sufficiently selective so as to minimize waste, discards, catch of non-target species, both fish and non-fish species, and impacts on associated or dependent species and that the intent of related regulations is not circumvented by technical devices. In this regard, fishers should cooperate in the development of selective fishing gear and methods. States should ensure that information on new developments and requirements is made available to all fishers.
8.5.2   In order to improve selectivity, States should, when drawing up their laws and regulations, take into account the range of selective fishing gear, methods and strategies available to the industry.
8.5.3   States and relevant institutions should collaborate in developing standard methodologies for research into fishing gear selectivity, fishing methods and strategies.
8.5.4   International cooperation should be encouraged with respect to research programmes for fishing gear selectivity, and fishing methods and strategies, dissemination of the results of such research programmes and the transfer of technology.

8.6   *Energy optimization*

8.6.1   States should promote the development of appropriate standards and guidelines which would lead to the more efficient use of energy in harvesting and post-harvest activities within the fisheries sector.
8.6.2   States should promote the development and transfer of technology in relation to energy optimization within the fisheries sector and, in particular, encourage owners, charterers and managers of fishing vessels to fit energy optimization devices to their vessels.

8.7   *Protection of the aquatic environment*

8.7.1   States should introduce and enforce laws and regulations based on the International Convention for the Prevention of Pollution from Ships, 1973, as modified by the Protocol of 1978 relating thereto (MARPOL 73/78).
8.7.2   Owners, charterers and managers of fishing vessels should ensure that their vessels are fitted with appropriate equipment as required by MARPOL 73/78 and should consider fitting a shipboard compactor or incinerator to relevant classes of vessels in order to treat garbage and other shipboard wastes generated during the vessel's normal service.
8.7.3   Owners, charterers and managers of fishing vessels should minimize the taking aboard of potential garbage through proper provisioning practices.
8.7.4   The crew of fishing vessels should be conversant with proper shipboard procedures in order to ensure discharges do not exceed the levels set by MARPOL 73/78. Such procedures should, as a minimum, include the disposal of oily waste and the handling and storage of shipboard garbage.

8.8   Protection of the atmosphere

8.8.1   States should adopt relevant standards and guidelines which would include provisions for the reduction of dangerous substances in exhaust gas emissions.

8.8.2   Owners, charterers and managers of fishing vessels should ensure that their vessels are fitted with equipment to reduce emissions of ozone depleting substances. The responsible crew members of fishing vessels should be conversant with the proper running and maintenance of machinery on board.

8.8.3   Competent authorities should make provision for the phasing out of the use of chlorofluorocarbons (CFCs) and transitional substances such as hydrochlorofluorocarbons (HCFCs) in the refrigeration systems of fishing vessels and should ensure that the shipbuilding industry and those engaged in the fishing industry are informed of and comply with such provisions.

8.8.4   Owners or managers of fishing vessels should take appropriate action to refit existing vessels with alternative refrigerants to CFCs and HCFCs and alternatives to Halons in fire fighting installations. Such alternatives should be used in specifications for all new fishing vessels.

8.8.5   States and owners, charterers and managers of fishing vessels as well as fishers should follow international guidelines for the disposal of CFCs, HCFCs and Halons.

8.9   Harbours and landing places for fishing vessels

8.9.1   States should take into account, inter alia, the following in the design and construction of harbours and landing places:

(a)   safe havens for fishing vessels and adequate servicing facilities for vessels, vendors and buyers are provided;

(b)   adequate freshwater supplies and sanitation arrangements should be provided;

(c)   waste disposal systems should be introduced, including for the disposal of oil, oily water and fishing gear;

(d)   pollution from fisheries activities and external sources should be minimized; and

(e)   arrangements should be made to combat the effects of erosion and siltation.

8.9.2   States should establish an institutional framework for the selection or improvement of sites for harbours for fishing vessels which allows for consultation among the authorities responsible for coastal area management.

8.10   Abandonment of structures and other materials

8.10.1   States should ensure that the standards and guidelines for the removal of redundant offshore structures issued by the International Maritime Organization are followed. States should also ensure that the competent fisheries authorities are consulted prior to decisions being made on the abandonment of structures and other materials by the relevant authorities.

8.11   Artificial reefs and fish aggregation devices

8.11.1   States, where appropriate, should develop policies for increasing stock populations and enhancing fishing opportunities through the use of artificial structures, placed with due regard to the safety of navigation, on or above the seabed or at the surface. Research into the use of such structures, including the impacts on living marine resources and the environment, should be promoted.

8.11.2   States should ensure that, when selecting the materials to be used in the creation of artificial reefs as well as when selecting the geographical location of such artificial reefs, the provisions of relevant international conventions concerning the environment and safety of navigation are observed.

8.11.3   States should, within the framework of coastal area management plans, establish management systems for artificial reefs and fish aggregation devices.   Such management systems should require approval for the construction and deployment of such reefs and devices and should take into account the interests of fishers, including artisanal and subsistence fishers.

8.11.4   States should ensure that the authorities responsible for maintaining cartographic records and charts for the purpose of navigation, as well as relevant environmental authorities, are informed prior to the placement or removal of artificial reefs or fish aggregation devices.

ARTICLE 9 - AQUACULTURE DEVELOPMENT

9.1   Responsible development of aquaculture, including culture-based fisheries, in areas under national jurisdiction

9.1.1   States should establish, maintain and develop an appropriate legal and administrative framework which facilitates the development of responsible aquaculture.

9.1.2   States should promote responsible development and management of aquaculture, including an advance evaluation of the effects of aquaculture development on genetic diversity and ecosystem integrity, based on the best available scientific information.

9.1.3   States should produce and regularly update aquaculture development strategies and plans, as required, to ensure that aquaculture development is ecologically sustainable and to allow the rational use of resources shared by aquaculture and other activities.

9.1.4   States should ensure that the livelihoods of local communities, and their access to fishing grounds, are not negatively affected by aquaculture developments.

9.1.5   States should establish effective procedures specific to aquaculture to undertake appropriate environmental assessment and monitoring with the aim of minimizing adverse ecological changes and related economic and social consequences resulting from water extraction, land use, discharge of effluents, use of drugs and chemicals, and other aquaculture activities.

9.2   Responsible development of aquaculture including culture-based fisheries within transboundary aquatic ecosystems

9.2.1   States should protect transboundary aquatic ecosystems by supporting responsible aquaculture practices within their national jurisdiction and by cooperation in the promotion of sustainable aquaculture practices.

9.2.2   States should, with due respect to their neighbouring States, and in accordance with international law, ensure responsible choice of species, siting and management of aquaculture activities which could affect transboundary aquatic ecosystems.

9.2.3   States should consult with their neighbouring States, as appropriate, before introducing non-indigenous species into transboundary aquatic ecosystems.

9.2.4   States should establish appropriate mechanisms, such as databases and information networks to collect, share and disseminate data related to their aquaculture activities to facilitate cooperation on planning for aquaculture development at the national, subregional, regional and global level.
9.2.5   States should cooperate in the development of appropriate mechanisms, when required, to monitor the impacts of inputs used in aquaculture.

9.3   Use of aquatic genetic resources for the purposes of aquaculture including culture-based fisheries

9.3.1   States should conserve genetic diversity and maintain integrity of aquatic communities and ecosystems by appropriate management. In particular, efforts should be undertaken to minimize the harmful effects of introducing non-native species or genetically altered stocks used for aquaculture including culture-based fisheries into waters, especially where there is a significant potential for the spread of such non-native species or genetically altered stocks into waters under the jurisdiction of other States as well as waters under the jurisdiction of the State of origin. States should, whenever possible, promote steps to minimize adverse genetic, disease and other effects of escaped farmed fish on wild stocks.
9.3.2   States should cooperate in the elaboration, adoption and implementation of international codes of practice and procedures for introductions and transfers of aquatic organisms.
9.3.3   States should, in order to minimize risks of disease transfer and other adverse effects on wild and cultured stocks, encourage adoption of appropriate practices in the genetic improvement of broodstocks, the introduction of non-native species, and in the production, sale and transport of eggs, larvae or fry, broodstock or other live materials. States should facilitate the preparation and implementation of appropriate national codes of practice and procedures to this effect.
9.3.4   States should promote the use of appropriate procedures for the selection of broodstock and the production of eggs, larvae and fry.
9.3.5   States should, where appropriate, promote research and, when feasible, the development of culture techniques for endangered species to protect, rehabilitate and enhance their stocks, taking into account the critical need to conserve genetic diversity of endangered species.

9.4   Responsible aquaculture at the production level

9.4.1   States should promote responsible aquaculture practices in support of rural communities, producer organizations and fish farmers.
9.4.2   States should promote active participation of fishfarmers and their communities in the development of responsible aquaculture management practices.
9.4.3   States should promote efforts which improve selection and use of appropriate feeds, feed additives and fertilizers, including manures.
9.4.4   States should promote effective farm and fish health management practices favouring hygienic measures and vaccines. Safe, effective and minimal use of therapeutants, hormones and drugs, antibiotics and other disease control chemicals should be ensured.
9.4.5   States should regulate the use of chemical inputs in aquaculture which are hazardous to human health and the environment.
9.4.6   States should require that the disposal of wastes such as offal, sludge, dead or diseased fish, excess veterinary drugs and other hazardous

chemical inputs does not constitute a hazard to human health and the environment.

9.4.7 States should ensure the food safety of aquaculture products and promote efforts which maintain product quality and improve their value through particular care before and during harvesting and on-site processing and in storage and transport of the products.

ARTICLE 10 - INTEGRATION OF FISHERIES INTO COASTAL AREA MANAGEMENT

10.1 Institutional framework

10.1.1 States should ensure that an appropriate policy, legal and institutional framework is adopted to achieve the sustainable and integrated use of the resources, taking into account the fragility of coastal ecosystems and the finite nature of their natural resources and the needs of coastal communities.

10.1.2 In view of the multiple uses of the coastal area, States should ensure that representatives of the fisheries sector and fishing communities are consulted in the decision-making processes and involved in other activities related to coastal area management planning and development.

10.1.3 States should develop, as appropriate, institutional and legal frameworks in order to determine the possible uses of coastal resources and to govern access to them taking into account the rights of coastal fishing communities and their customary practices to the extent compatible with sustainable development.

10.1.4 States should facilitate the adoption of fisheries practices that avoid conflict among fisheries resources users and between them and other users of the coastal area.

10.1.5 States should promote the establishment of procedures and mechanisms at the appropriate administrative level to settle conflicts which arise within the fisheries sector and between fisheries resource users and other users of the coastal area.

10.2 Policy measures

10.2.1 States should promote the creation of public awareness of the need for the protection and management of coastal resources and the participation in the management process by those affected.

10.2.2 In order to assist decision-making on the allocation and use of coastal resources, States should promote the assessment of their respective value taking into account economic, social and cultural factors.

10.2.3 In setting policies for the management of coastal areas, States should take due account of the risks and uncertainties involved.

10.2.4 States, in accordance with their capacities, should establish or promote the establishment of systems to monitor the coastal environment as part of the coastal management process using physical, chemical, biological, economic and social parameters.

10.2.5 States should promote multi-disciplinary research in support of coastal area management, in particular on its environmental, biological, economic, social, legal and institutional aspects.

10.3   *Regional cooperation*

10.3.1   States with neighbouring coastal areas should cooperate with one another to facilitate the sustainable use of coastal resources and the conservation of the environment.
10.3.2   In the case of activities that may have an adverse transboundary environmental effect on coastal areas, States should:
      (a)   provide timely information and, if possible, prior notification to potentially affected States; and
      (b)   consult with those States as early as possible.
10.3.3   States should cooperate at the subregional and regional level in order to improve coastal area management.

10.4   *Implementation*

10.4.1   States should establish mechanisms for cooperation and coordination among national authorities involved in planning, development, conservation and management of coastal areas.
10.4.2   States should ensure that the authority or authorities representing the fisheries sector in the coastal management process have the appropriate technical capacities and financial resources.

ARTICLE 11 - POST-HARVEST PRACTICES AND TRADE

11.1   *Responsible fish utilization*

11.1.1   States should adopt appropriate measures to ensure the right of consumers to safe, wholesome and unadulterated fish and fishery products.
11.1.2   States should establish and maintain effective national safety and quality assurance systems to protect consumer health and prevent commercial fraud.
11.1.3   States should set minimum standards for safety and quality assurance and make sure that these standards are effectively applied throughout the industry. They should promote the implementation of quality standards agreed within the context of the FAO/WHO Codex Alimentarius Commission and other relevant organizations or arrangements.
11.1.4   States should cooperate to achieve harmonization, or mutual recognition, or both, of national sanitary measures and certification programmes as appropriate and explore possibilities for the establishment of mutually recognized control and certification agencies.
11.1.5   States should give due consideration to the economic and social role of the post-harvest fisheries sector when formulating national policies for the sustainable development and utilization of fishery resources.
11.1.6   States and relevant organizations should sponsor research in fish technology and quality assurance and support projects to improve post-harvest handling of fish, taking into account the economic, social, environmental and nutritional impact of such projects.
11.1.7   States, noting the existence of different production methods, should through cooperation and by facilitating the development and transfer of appropriate technologies, ensure that processing, transporting and storage methods are environmentally sound.

11.1.8 States should encourage those involved in fish processing, distribution and marketing to:
    (a)   reduce post-harvest losses and waste;
    (b)   improve the use of by-catch to the extent that this is consistent with responsible fisheries management practices; and
    (c)   use the resources, especially water and energy, in particular wood, in an environmentally sound manner.
11.1.9 States should encourage the use of fish for human consumption and promote consumption of fish whenever appropriate.
11.1.10 States should cooperate in order to facilitate the production of value-added products by developing countries.
11.1.11 States should ensure that international and domestic trade in fish and fishery products accords with sound conservation and management practices through improving the identification of the origin of fish and fishery products traded.
11.1.12 States should ensure that environmental effects of post-harvest activities are considered in the development of related laws, regulations and policies without creating any market distortions.

11.2   Responsible international trade

11.2.1 The provisions of this Code should be interpreted and applied in accordance with the principles, rights and obligations established in the World Trade Organization (WTO) Agreement.
11.2.2 International trade in fish and fishery products should not compromise the sustainable development of fisheries and responsible utilization of living aquatic resources.
11.2.3 States should ensure that measures affecting international trade in fish and fishery products are transparent, based, when applicable, on scientific evidence, and are in accordance with internationally agreed rules.
11.2.4 Fish trade measures adopted by States to protect human or animal life or health, the interests of consumers or the environment, should not be discriminatory and should be in accordance with internationally agreed trade rules, in particular the principles, rights and obligations established in the Agreement on the Application of Sanitary and Phytosanitary Measures and the Agreement on Technical Barriers to Trade of the WTO.
11.2.5 States should further liberalize trade in fish and fishery products and eliminate barriers and distortions to trade such as duties, quotas and non-tariff barriers in accordance with the principles, rights and obligations of the WTO Agreement.
11.2.6 States should not directly or indirectly create unnecessary or hidden barriers to trade which limit the consumer's freedom of choice of supplier or that restrict market access.
11.2.7 States should not condition access to markets to access to resources. This principle does not preclude the possibility of fishing agreements between States which include provisions referring to access to resources, trade and access to markets, transfer of technology, scientific research, training and other relevant elements.
11.2.8 States should not link access to markets to the purchase of specific technology or sale of other products.
11.2.9 States should cooperate in complying with relevant international agreements regulating trade in endangered species.
11.2.10 States should develop international agreements for trade in live specimens where there is a risk of environmental damage in importing or exporting States.

11.2.11 States should cooperate to promote adherence to, and effective implementation of relevant international standards for trade in fish and fishery products and living aquatic resource conservation.
11.2.12 States should not undermine conservation measures for living aquatic resources in order to gain trade or investment benefits.
11.2.13 States should cooperate to develop internationally acceptable rules or standards for trade in fish and fishery products in accordance with the principles, rights, and obligations established in the WTO Agreement.
11.2.14 States should cooperate with each other and actively participate in relevant regional and multilateral fora, such as the WTO, in order to ensure equitable, non-discriminatory trade in fish and fishery products as well as wide adherence to multilaterally agreed fishery conservation measures.
11.2.15 States, aid agencies, multilateral development banks and other relevant international organizations should ensure that their policies and practices related to the promotion of international fish trade and export production do not result in environmental degradation or adversely impact the nutritional rights and needs of people for whom fish is critical to their health and well being and for whom other comparable sources of food are not readily available or affordable.

11.3 Laws and regulations relating to fish trade

11.3.1 Laws, regulations and administrative procedures applicable to international trade in fish and fishery products should be transparent, as simple as possible, comprehensible and, when appropriate, based on scientific evidence.
11.3.2 States, in accordance with their national laws, should facilitate appropriate consultation with and participation of industry as well as environmental and consumer groups in the development and implementation of laws and regulations related to trade in fish and fishery products.
11.3.3 States should simplify their laws, regulations and administrative procedures applicable to trade in fish and fishery products without jeopardizing their effectiveness.
11.3.4 When a State introduces changes to its legal requirements affecting trade in fish and fishery products with other States, sufficient information and time should be given to allow the States and producers affected to introduce, as appropriate, the changes needed in their processes and procedures. In this connection, consultation with affected States on the time frame for implementation of the changes would be desirable. Due consideration should be given to requests from developing countries for temporary derogations from obligations.
11.3.5 States should periodically review laws and regulations applicable to international trade in fish and fishery products in order to determine whether the conditions which gave rise to their introduction continue to exist.
11.3.6 States should harmonize as far as possible the standards applicable to international trade in fish and fishery products in accordance with relevant internationally recognized provisions.
11.3.7 States should collect, disseminate and exchange timely, accurate and pertinent statistical information on international trade in fish and fishery products through relevant national institutions and international organizations.
11.3.8 States should promptly notify interested States, WTO and other appropriate international organizations on the development of and changes to laws, regulations and administrative procedures applicable to international trade in fish and fishery products.

ARTICLE 12 - FISHERIES RESEARCH

12.1   States should recognize that responsible fisheries requires the availability of a sound scientific basis to assist fisheries managers and other interested parties in making decisions. Therefore, States should ensure that appropriate research is conducted into all aspects of fisheries including biology, ecology, technology, environmental science, economics, social science, aquaculture and nutritional science. States should ensure the availability of research facilities and provide appropriate training, staffing and institution building to conduct the research, taking into account the special needs of developing countries.

12.2   States should establish an appropriate institutional framework to determine the applied research which is required and its proper use.

12.3   States should ensure that data generated by research are analyzed, that the results of such analyses are published, respecting confidentiality where appropriate, and distributed in a timely and readily understood fashion, in order that the best scientific evidence is made available as a contribution to fisheries conservation, management and development. In the absence of adequate scientific information, appropriate research should be initiated as soon as possible.

12.4   States should collect reliable and accurate data which are required to assess the status of fisheries and ecosystems, including data on bycatch, discards and waste. Where appropriate, this data should be provided, at an appropriate time and level of aggregation, to relevant States and subregional, regional and global fisheries organizations.

12.5   States should be able to monitor and assess the state of the stocks under their jurisdiction, including the impacts of ecosystem changes resulting from fishing pressure, pollution or habitat alteration. They should also establish the research capacity necessary to assess the effects of climate or environment change on fish stocks and aquatic ecosystems.

12.6   States should support and strengthen national research capabilities to meet acknowledged scientific standards.

12.7   States, as appropriate in cooperation with relevant international organizations, should encourage research to ensure optimum utilization of fishery resources and stimulate the research required to support national policies related to fish as food.

12.8   States should conduct research into, and monitor, human food supplies from aquatic sources and the environment from which they are taken and ensure that there is no adverse health impact on consumers. The results of such research should be made publicly available.

12.9   States should ensure that the economic, social, marketing and institutional aspects of fisheries are adequately researched and that comparable data are generated for ongoing monitoring, analysis and policy formulation.

12.10   States should carry out studies on the selectivity of fishing gear, the environmental impact of fishing gear on target species and on the behaviour of target and non-target species in relation to such fishing gear as an aid for management decisions and with a view to minimizing non-utilized catches as well as safeguarding the biodiversity of ecosystems and the aquatic habitat.

12.11   States should ensure that before the commercial introduction of new types of gear, a scientific evaluation of their impact on the fisheries and ecosystems where they will be used should be undertaken. The effects of such gear introductions should be monitored.

12.12   States should investigate and document traditional fisheries knowledge and technologies, in particular those applied to small-scale fisheries, in order to assess their application to sustainable fisheries conservation, management and development.

12.13   States should promote the use of research results as a basis for the setting of management objectives, reference points and performance criteria, as well as for ensuring adequate linkages between applied research and fisheries management.

12.14   States conducting scientific research activities in waters under the jurisdiction of another State should ensure that their vessels comply with the laws and regulations of that State and international law.

12.15   States should promote the adoption of uniform guidelines governing fisheries research conducted on the high seas.

12.16   States should, where appropriate, support the establishment of mechanisms, including, inter alia, the adoption of uniform guidelines, to facilitate research at the subregional or regional level and should encourage the sharing of the results of such research with other regions.

12.17   States, either directly or with the support of relevant international organizations, should develop collaborative technical and research programmes to improve understanding of the biology, environment and status of transboundary aquatic stocks.

12.18   States and relevant international organizations should promote and enhance the research capacities of developing countries, inter alia, in the areas of data collection and analysis, information, science and technology, human resource development and provision of research facilities, in order for them to participate effectively in the conservation, management and sustainable use of living aquatic resources.

12.19   Competent international organizations should, where appropriate, render technical and financial support to States upon request and when engaged in research investigations aimed at evaluating stocks which have been previously unfished or very lightly fished.

12.20   Relevant technical and financial international organizations should, upon request, support States in their research efforts, devoting special attention to developing countries, in particular the least-developed among them and small island developing countries.

INDEX

Index
to International fisheries instruments
(Agreement for the Implementation of the Provisions of the United Nations Convention on the Law of the Sea of 10 December 1982 relating to the Conservation and Management of Straddling Fish Stocks and Highly Migratory Fish Stocks; Agreement to Promote Compliance with International Conservation and Management Measures by Fishing Vessels on the High Seas; Code of Conduct for Responsible Fisheries)

Nomenclature used in the index

Citations to the Agreement for the Implementation of the Provisions of the United Nations Convention on the Law of the Sea of 10 December 1982 relating to the Conservation and Management of Straddling Fish Stocks and Highly Migratory Fish Stocks are preceded by the letter **A**; citations to the Agreement to Promote Compliance with International Conservation and Management Measures by Fishing Vessels on the High Seas are indicated by the letters **CA**; and citations to the Code of Conduct for Responsible Fisheries are indicated by the letter **C**.

Citations to the *preambles to the two Agreements* refer to the relevant paragraph of the respective preamble, e.g., *Preamble* 8 denotes the eighth paragraph of the preamble. Citations to the Introduction to the Code of Conduct are designated by the word "Intro".

Citations to *articles* in the body of the instruments are given by the corresponding article number, paragraph, subparagraph, e.g., 18(3)(g)(i) denotes article 18, paragraph 3, subparagraph (g), sub-subparagraph (i), of the Fish Stocks Agreement; XV(c)(iii) denotes article XV, paragraph (c) subparagraph (iii), of the Compliance Agreement; or, similarly, 11.1.8(c) denotes article 11, paragraph 1, subparagraph 8, sub-subparagraph (c), of the Code of Conduct.

Citations to articles in *Annexes I and II* to the Fish Stocks Agreement are designated by an upper-case "A" followed by the number of the annex and the article, paragraph and subparagraph, as appropriate, e.g., (AI)5(3)(a) denotes Annex I, article 5, paragraph 3, subparagraph (a).

The expression "occurrence of the term" is used to denote instances where a specific word or term appears in the Convention, the Agreement, annexes or resolutions; in these instances there are no subdivisions into substantive classifications.

The expression "use of the term" generally signifies the definition of that word or term as used in the Convention, the Agreement, annexes or resolutions.

If a term occurs only in the title or in all paragraphs of an article, only the article number may be given.

ANNEX
Selected provisions of the United Nations Convention on the Law of
the Sea of 10 December 1982 relating to the conservation and
management of living marine resources

PART V

EXCLUSIVE ECONOMIC ZONE

Article 55
Specific legal regime of the exclusive economic zone

The exclusive economic zone is an area beyond and adjacent to the
territorial sea, subject to the specific legal regime established in this Part,
under which the rights and jurisdiction of the coastal State and the rights and
freedoms of other States are governed by the relevant provisions of this
Convention.

Article 56
*Rights, jurisdiction and duties of the coastal State in the exclusive
economic zone*

1. In the exclusive economic zone, the coastal State has:
    (a) sovereign rights for the purpose of exploring and exploiting,
         conserving and managing the natural resources, whether living
         or non-living, of the waters superjacent to the seabed and of
         the seabed and its subsoil, and with regard to other activities
         for the economic exploitation and exploration of the zone, such
         as the production of energy from the water, currents and
         winds;
    (b) jurisdiction as provided for in the relevant provisions of this
         Convention with regard to:
         (i)   the establishment and use of artificial islands,
                installations and structures;
         (ii)   marine scientific research;
         (iii) the protection and preservation of the marine
                environment;
    (c) other rights and duties provided for in this Convention.
2. In exercising its rights and performing its duties under this
Convention in the exclusive economic zone, the coastal State shall have due
regard to the rights and duties of other States and shall act in a manner
compatible with the provisions of this Convention.
3. The rights set out in this article with respect to the seabed and
subsoil shall be exercised in accordance with Part VI.

Article 57
Breadth of the exclusive economic zone

The exclusive economic zone shall not extend beyond 200 nautical miles
from the baselines from which the breadth of the territorial sea is measured.

Article 58
Rights and duties of other States in the exclusive economic zone

1. In the exclusive economic zone, all States, whether coastal or land-locked, enjoy, subject to the relevant provisions of this Convention, the freedoms referred to in article 87 of navigation and overflight and of the laying of submarine cables and pipelines, and other internationally lawful uses of the sea related to these freedoms, such as those associated with the operation of ships, aircraft and submarine cables and pipelines, and compatible with the other provisions of this Convention.
2. Articles 88 to 115 and other pertinent rules of international law apply to the exclusive economic zone in so far as they are not incompatible with this Part.
3. In exercising their rights and performing their duties under this Convention in the exclusive economic zone, States shall have due regard to the rights and duties of the coastal State and shall comply with the laws and regulations adopted by the coastal State in accordance with the provisions of this Convention and other rules of international law in so far as they are not incompatible with this Part.

Article 59
Basis for the resolution of conflicts
regarding the attribution of rights and jurisdiction
in the exclusive economic zone

In cases where this Convention does not attribute rights or jurisdiction to the coastal State or to other States within the exclusive economic zone, and a conflict arises between the interests of the coastal State and any other State or States, the conflict should be resolved on the basis of equity and in the light of all the relevant circumstances, taking into account the respective importance of the interests involved to the parties as well as to the international community as a whole.

Article 60
Artificial islands, installations and structures
in the exclusive economic zone

1. In the exclusive economic zone, the coastal State shall have the exclusive right to construct and to authorize and regulate the construction, operation and use of:
    (a) artificial islands;
    (b) installations and structures for the purposes provided for in article 56 and other economic purposes;
    (c) installations and structures which may interfere with the exercise of the rights of the coastal State in the zone.
2. The coastal State shall have exclusive jurisdiction over such artificial islands, installations and structures, including jurisdiction with regard to customs, fiscal, health, safety and immigration laws and regulations.
3. Due notice must be given of the construction of such artificial islands, installations or structures, and permanent means for giving warning of their presence must be maintained. Any installations or structures which are abandoned or disused shall be removed to ensure safety of navigation, taking into account any generally accepted international standards established in this regard by the competent international organization. Such removal shall also have due regard to fishing, the protection of the marine environment and the rights and duties of other States. Appropriate publicity

shall be given to the depth, position and dimensions of any installations or structures not entirely removed.

4. The coastal State may, where necessary, establish reasonable safety zones around such artificial islands, installations and structures in which it may take appropriate measures to ensure the safety both of navigation and of the artificial islands, installations and structures.

5. The breadth of the safety zones shall be determined by the coastal State, taking into account applicable international standards. Such zones shall be designed to ensure that they are reasonably related to the nature and function of the artificial islands, installations or structures, and shall not exceed a distance of 500 metres around them, measured from each point of their outer edge, except as authorized by generally accepted international standards or as recommended by the competent international organization. Due notice shall be given of the extent of safety zones.

6. All ships must respect these safety zones and shall comply with generally accepted international standards regarding navigation in the vicinity of artificial islands, installations, structures and safety zones.

7. Artificial islands, installations and structures and the safety zones around them may not be established where interference may be caused to the use of recognized sea lanes essential to international navigation.

8. Artificial islands, installations and structures do not possess the status of islands. They have no territorial sea of their own, and their presence does not affect the delimitation of the territorial sea, the exclusive economic zone or the continental shelf.

Article 61
Conservation of the living resources

1. The coastal State shall determine the allowable catch of the living resources in its exclusive economic zone.

2. The coastal State, taking into account the best scientific evidence available to it, shall ensure through proper conservation and management measures that the maintenance of the living resources in the exclusive economic zone is not endangered by over-exploitation. As appropriate, the coastal State and competent international organizations, whether subregional, regional or global, shall cooperate to this end.

3. Such measures shall also be designed to maintain or restore populations of harvested species at levels which can produce the maximum sustainable yield, as qualified by relevant environmental and economic factors, including the economic needs of coastal fishing communities and the special requirements of developing States, and taking into account fishing patterns, the interdependence of stocks and any generally recommended international minimum standards, whether subregional, regional or global.

4. In taking such measures the coastal State shall take into consideration the effects on species associated with or dependent upon harvested species with a view to maintaining or restoring populations of such associated or dependent species above levels at which their reproduction may become seriously threatened.

5. Available scientific information, catch and fishing effort statistics, and other data relevant to the conservation of fish stocks shall be contributed and exchanged on a regular basis through competent international organizations, whether subregional, regional or global, where appropriate and with participation by all States concerned, including States whose nationals are allowed to fish in the exclusive economic zone.

Article 62
Utilization of the living resources

1. The coastal State shall promote the objective of optimum utilization of the living resources in the exclusive economic zone without prejudice to article 61.
2. The coastal State shall determine its capacity to harvest the living resources of the exclusive economic zone. Where the coastal State does not have the capacity to harvest the entire allowable catch, it shall, through agreements or other arrangements and pursuant to the terms, conditions, laws and regulations referred to in paragraph 4, give other States access to the surplus of the allowable catch, having particular regard to the provisions of articles 69 and 70, especially in relation to the developing States mentioned therein.
3. In giving access to other States to its exclusive economic zone under this article, the coastal State shall take into account all relevant factors, including, *inter alia*, the significance of the living resources of the area to the economy of the coastal State concerned and its other national interests, the provisions of articles 69 and 70, the requirements of developing States in the subregion or region in harvesting part of the surplus and the need to minimize economic dislocation in States whose nationals have habitually fished in the zone or which have made substantial efforts in research and identification of stocks.
4. Nationals of other States fishing in the exclusive economic zone shall comply with the conservation measures and with the other terms and conditions established in the laws and regulations of the coastal State. These laws and regulations shall be consistent with this Convention and may relate, *inter alia*, to the following:
    (a) licensing of fishermen, fishing vessels and equipment, including payment of fees and other forms of remuneration, which, in the case of developing coastal States, may consist of adequate compensation in the field of financing, equipment and technology relating to the fishing industry;
    (b) determining the species which may be caught, and fixing quotas of catch, whether in relation to particular stocks or groups of stocks or catch per vessel over a period of time or to the catch by nationals of any State during a specified period;
    (c) regulating seasons and areas of fishing, the types, sizes and amount of gear, and the types, sizes and number of fishing vessels that may be used;
    (d) fixing the age and size of fish and other species that may be caught;
    (e) specifying information required of fishing vessels, including catch and effort statistics and vessel position reports;
    (f) requiring, under the authorization and control of the coastal State, the conduct of specified fisheries research programmes and regulating the conduct of such research, including the sampling of catches, disposition of samples and reporting of associated scientific data;
    (g) the placing of observers or trainees on board such vessels by the coastal State;
    (h) the landing of all or any part of the catch by such vessels in the ports of the coastal State;
    (i) terms and conditions relating to joint ventures or other ooperative arrangements;

(j) requirements for the training of personnel and the transfer of fisheries technology, including enhancement of the coastal State's capability of undertaking fisheries research;
(k) enforcement procedures.
5.   Coastal States shall give due notice of conservation and management laws and regulations.

Article 63
Stocks occurring within the exclusive economic zones of
two or more coastal States or both within the exclusive economic zone
and in an area beyond and adjacent to it

1.   Where the same stock or stocks of associated species occur within the exclusive economic zones of two or more coastal States, these States shall seek, either directly or through appropriate subregional or regional organizations, to agree upon the measures necessary to coordinate and ensure the conservation and development of such stocks without prejudice to the other provisions of this Part.
2.   Where the same stock or stocks of associated species occur both within the exclusive economic zone and in an area beyond and adjacent to the zone, the coastal State and the States fishing for such stocks in the adjacent area shall seek, either directly or through appropriate subregional or regional organizations, to agree upon the measures necessary for the conservation of these stocks in the adjacent area.

Article 64
Highly migratory species

1.   The coastal State and other States whose nationals fish in the region for the highly migratory species listed in Annex I shall cooperate directly or through appropriate international organizations with a view to ensuring conservation and promoting the objective of optimum utilization of such species throughout the region, both within and beyond the exclusive economic zone. In regions for which no appropriate international organization exists, the coastal State and other States whose nationals harvest these species in the region shall cooperate to establish such an organization and participate in its work.
2.   The provisions of paragraph 1 apply in addition to the other provisions of this Part.

Article 65
Marine mammals

Nothing in this Part restricts the right of a coastal State or the competence of an international organization, as appropriate, to prohibit, limit or regulate the exploitation of marine mammals more strictly than provided for in this Part. States shall cooperate with a view to the conservation of marine mammals and in the case of cetaceans shall in particular work through the appropriate international organizations for their conservation, management and study.

Article 66
Anadromous stocks

1.   States in whose rivers anadromous stocks originate shall have the primary interest in and responsibility for such stocks.

2.   The State of origin of anadromous stocks shall ensure their conservation by the establishment of appropriate regulatory measures for fishing in all waters landward of the outer limits of its exclusive economic zone and for fishing provided for in paragraph 3(b). The State of origin may, after consultations with the other States referred to in paragraphs 3 and 4 fishing these stocks, establish total allowable catches for stocks originating in its rivers.

3.   (a) Fisheries for anadromous stocks shall be conducted only in waters landward of the outer limits of exclusive economic zones, except in cases where this provision would result in economic dislocation for a State other than the State of origin. With respect to such fishing beyond the outer limits of the exclusive economic zone, States concerned shall maintain consultations with a view to achieving agreement on terms and conditions of such fishing giving due regard to the conservation requirements and the needs of the State of origin in respect of these stocks.

(b) The State of origin shall cooperate in minimizing economic dislocation in such other States fishing these stocks, taking into account the normal catch and the mode of operations of such States, and all the areas in which such fishing has occurred.

(c) States referred to in subparagraph (b), participating by agreement with the State of origin in measures to renew anadromous stocks, particularly by expenditures for that purpose, shall be given special consideration by the State of origin in the harvesting of stocks originating in its rivers.

(d) Enforcement of regulations regarding anadromous stocks beyond the exclusive economic zone shall be by agreement between the State of origin and the other States concerned.

4.   In cases where anadromous stocks migrate into or through the waters landward of the outer limits of the exclusive economic zone of a State other than the State of origin, such State shall cooperate with the State of origin with regard to the conservation and management of such stocks.

5.   The State of origin of anadromous stocks and other States fishing these stocks shall make arrangements for the implementation of the provisions of this article, where appropriate, through regional organizations.

Article 67
Catadromous species

1.   A coastal State in whose waters catadromous species spend the greater part of their life cycle shall have responsibility for the management of these species and shall ensure the ingress and egress of migrating fish.

2.   Harvesting of catadromous species shall be conducted only in waters landward of the outer limits of exclusive economic zones. When conducted in exclusive economic zones, harvesting shall be subject to this article and the other provisions of this Convention concerning fishing in these zones.

3.   In cases where catadromous fish migrate through the exclusive economic zone of another State, whether as juvenile or maturing fish, the management, including harvesting, of such fish shall be regulated by agreement between the State mentioned in paragraph 1 and the other State

concerned. Such agreement shall ensure the rational management of the species and take into account the responsibilities of the State mentioned in paragraph 1 for the maintenance of these species.

Article 68
Sedentary species

This Part does not apply to sedentary species as defined in article 77, paragraph 4.

Article 69
Right of land-locked States

1. Land-locked States shall have the right to participate, on an equitable basis, in the exploitation of an appropriate part of the surplus of the living resources of the exclusive economic zones of coastal States of the same subregion or region, taking into account the relevant economic and geographical circumstances of all the States concerned and in conformity with the provisions of this article and of articles 61 and 62.

2. The terms and modalities of such participation shall be established by the States concerned through bilateral, subregional or regional agreements taking into account, *inter alia*:

    (a) the need to avoid effects detrimental to fishing communities or fishing industries of the coastal State;

    (b) the extent to which the land-locked State, in accordance with the provisions of this article, is participating or is entitled to participate under existing bilateral, subregional or regional agreements in the exploitation of living resources of the exclusive economic zones of other coastal States;

    (c) the extent to which other land-locked States and geographically disadvantaged States are participating in the exploitation of the living resources of the exclusive economic zone of the coastal State and the consequent need to avoid a particular burden for any single coastal State or a part of it;

    (d) the nutritional needs of the populations of the respective States.

3. When the harvesting capacity of a coastal State approaches a point which would enable it to harvest the entire allowable catch of the living resources in its exclusive economic zone, the coastal State and other States concerned shall cooperate in the establishment of equitable arrangements on a bilateral, subregional or regional basis to allow for participation of developing land-locked States of the same subregion or region in the exploitation of the living resources of the exclusive economic zones of coastal States of the subregion or region, as may be appropriate in the circumstances and on terms satisfactory to all parties. In the implementation of this provision the factors mentioned in paragraph 2 shall also be taken into account.

4. Developed land-locked States shall, under the provisions of this article, be entitled to participate in the exploitation of living resources only in the exclusive economic zones of developed coastal States of the same subregion or region having regard to the extent to which the coastal State, in giving access to other States to the living resources of its exclusive economic zone, has taken into account the need to minimize detrimental effects on fishing communities and economic dislocation in States whose nationals have habitually fished in the zone.

5. The above provisions are without prejudice to arrangements agreed upon in subregions or regions where the coastal States may grant to

land-locked States of the same subregion or region equal or preferential rights for the exploitation of the living resources in the exclusive economic zones.

Article 70
Right of geographically disadvantaged States

1. Geographically disadvantaged States shall have the right to participate, on an equitable basis, in the exploitation of an appropriate part of the surplus of the living resources of the exclusive economic zones of coastal States of the same subregion or region, taking into account the relevant economic and geographical circumstances of all the States concerned and in conformity with the provisions of this article and of articles 61 and 62.

2. For the purposes of this Part, "geographically disadvantaged States" means coastal States, including States bordering enclosed or semi-enclosed seas, whose geographical situation makes them dependent upon the exploitation of the living resources of the exclusive economic zones of other States in the subregion or region for adequate supplies of fish for the nutritional purposes of their populations or parts thereof, and coastal States which can claim no exclusive economic zones of their own.

3. The terms and modalities of such participation shall be established by the States concerned through bilateral, subregional or regional agreements taking into account, *inter alia*:

(a) the need to avoid effects detrimental to fishing communities or fishing industries of the coastal State;

(b) the extent to which the geographically disadvantaged State, in accordance with the provisions of this article, is participating or is entitled to participate under existing bilateral, subregional or regional agreements in the exploitation of living resources of the exclusive economic zones of other coastal States;

(c) the extent to which other geographically disadvantaged States and land-locked States are participating in the exploitation of the living resources of the exclusive economic zone of the coastal State and the consequent need to avoid a particular burden for any single coastal State or a part of it;

(d) the nutritional needs of the populations of the respective States.

4. When the harvesting capacity of a coastal State approaches a point which would enable it to harvest the entire allowable catch of the living resources in its exclusive economic zone, the coastal State and other States concerned shall cooperate in the establishment of equitable arrangements on a bilateral, subregional or regional basis to allow for participation of developing geographically disadvantaged States of the same subregion or region in the exploitation of the living resources of the exclusive economic zones of coastal States of the subregion or region, as may be appropriate in the circumstances and on terms satisfactory to all parties. In the implementation of this provision the factors mentioned in paragraph 3 shall also be taken into account.

5. Developed geographically disadvantaged States shall, under the provisions of this article, be entitled to participate in the exploitation of living resources only in the exclusive economic zones of developed coastal States of the same subregion or region having regard to the extent to which the coastal State, in giving access to other States to the living resources of its exclusive economic zone, has taken into account the need to minimize detrimental effects on fishing communities and economic dislocation in States whose nationals have habitually fished in the zone.

6. The above provisions are without prejudice to arrangements agreed upon in subregions or regions where the coastal States may grant to geographically disadvantaged States of the same subregion or region equal or preferential rights for the exploitation of the living resources in the exclusive economic zones.

Article 71
Non-applicability of articles 69 and 70

The provisions of articles 69 and 70 do not apply in the case of a coastal State whose economy is overwhelmingly dependent on the exploitation of the living resources of its exclusive economic zone.

Article 72
Restrictions on transfer of rights

1. Rights provided under articles 69 and 70 to exploit living resources shall not be directly or indirectly transferred to third States or their nationals by lease or licence, by establishing joint ventures or in any other manner which has the effect of such transfer unless otherwise agreed by the States concerned.
2. The foregoing provision does not preclude the States concerned from obtaining technical or financial assistance from third States or international organizations in order to facilitate the exercise of the rights pursuant to articles 69 and 70, provided that it does not have the effect referred to in paragraph 1.

Article 73
Enforcement of laws and regulations of the coastal State

1. The coastal State may, in the exercise of its sovereign rights to explore, exploit, conserve and manage the living resources in the exclusive economic zone, take such measures, including boarding, inspection, arrest and judicial proceedings, as may be necessary to ensure compliance with the laws and regulations adopted by it in conformity with this Convention.
2. Arrested vessels and their crews shall be promptly released upon the posting of reasonable bond or other security.
3. Coastal State penalties for violations of fisheries laws and regulations in the exclusive economic zone may not include imprisonment, in the absence of agreements to the contrary by the States concerned, or any other form of corporal punishment.
4. In cases of arrest or detention of foreign vessels the coastal State shall promptly notify the flag State, through appropriate channels, of the action taken and of any penalties subsequently imposed.

Article 74
Delimitation of the exclusive economic zone
between States with opposite or adjacent coasts

1. The delimitation of the exclusive economic zone between States with opposite or adjacent coasts shall be effected by agreement on the basis of international law, as referred to in Article 38 of the Statute of the International Court of Justice, in order to achieve an equitable solution.
2. If no agreement can be reached within a reasonable period of time, the States concerned shall resort to the procedures provided for in Part XV.

3. Pending agreement as provided for in paragraph 1, the States concerned, in a spirit of understanding and cooperation, shall make every effort to enter into provisional arrangements of a practical nature and, during this transitional period, not to jeopardize or hamper the reaching of the final agreement. Such arrangements shall be without prejudice to the final delimitation.

4. Where there is an agreement in force between the States concerned, questions relating to the delimitation of the exclusive economic zone shall be determined in accordance with the provisions of that agreement.

Article 75
Charts and lists of geographical coordinates

1. Subject to this Part, the outer limit lines of the exclusive economic zone and the lines of delimitation drawn in accordance with article 74 shall be shown on charts of a scale or scales adequate for ascertaining their position. Where appropriate, lists of geographical coordinates of points, specifying the geodetic datum, may be substituted for such outer limit lines or lines of delimitation.

2. The coastal State shall give due publicity to such charts or lists of geographical coordinates and shall deposit a copy of each such chart or list with the Secretary-General of the United Nations.

...

PART VII

HIGH SEAS

...

SECTION 2. CONSERVATION AND MANAGEMENT OF THE LIVING RESOURCES OF THE HIGH SEAS

Article 116
Right to fish on the high seas

All States have the right for their nationals to engage in fishing on the high seas subject to:
(a) their treaty obligations;
(b) the rights and duties as well as the interests of coastal States provided for, *inter alia*, in article 63, paragraph 2, and articles 64 to 67; and
(c) the provisions of this section.

Article 117
Duty of States to adopt with respect to their nationals measures for the conservation of the living resources of the high seas

All States have the duty to take, or to cooperate with other States in taking, such measures for their respective nationals as may be necessary for the conservation of the living resources of the high seas.

Article 118
Cooperation of States in the conservation and management of living resources

States shall cooperate with each other in the conservation and management of living resources in the areas of the high seas. States whose nationals exploit identical living resources, or different living resources in the same area, shall enter into negotiations with a view to taking the measures necessary for the conservation of the living resources concerned. They shall, as appropriate, cooperate to establish subregional or regional fisheries organizations to this end.

Article 119
Conservation of the living resources of the high seas

1.   In determining the allowable catch and establishing other conservation measures for the living resources in the high seas, States shall:

(a)   take measures which are designed, on the best scientific evidence available to the States concerned, to maintain or restore populations of harvested species at levels which can produce the maximum sustainable yield, as qualified by relevant environmental and economic factors, including the special requirements of developing States, and taking into account fishing patterns, the interdependence of stocks and any generally recommended international minimum standards, whether subregional, regional or global;

(b)   take into consideration the effects on species associated with or dependent upon harvested species with a view to maintaining or restoring populations of such associated or dependent species above levels at which their reproduction may become seriously threatened.

2.   Available scientific information, catch and fishing effort statistics, and other data relevant to the conservation of fish stocks shall be contributed and exchanged on a regular basis through competent international organizations, whether subregional, regional or global, where appropriate and with participation by all States concerned.

3.   States concerned shall ensure that conservation measures and their implementation do not discriminate in form or in fact against the fishermen of any State.

Article 120
Marine mammals

Article 65 also applies to the conservation and management of marine mammals in the high seas.

كيفية الحصول على منشورات الأمم المتحدة

يمكن الحصول على منشورات الأمم المتحدة من المكتبات ودور التوزيع في جميع أنحاء العالم . استعلم عنها من المكتبة
التي تتعامل معها أو اكتب إلى : الأمم المتحدة ، قسم البيع في نيويورك أو في جنيف .

如何购取联合国出版物

联合国出版物在全世界各地的书店和经售处均有发售。请向书店询问或写信到纽约或日内瓦的
联合国销售组。

HOW TO OBTAIN UNITED NATIONS PUBLICATIONS

United Nations publications may be obtained from bookstores and distributors throughout the
world. Consult your bookstore or write to: United Nations, Sales Section, New York or Geneva.

COMMENT SE PROCURER LES PUBLICATIONS DES NATIONS UNIES

Les publications des Nations Unies sont en vente dans les librairies et les agences dépositaires
du monde entier. Informez-vous auprès de votre libraire ou adressez-vous à : Nations Unies,
Section des ventes, New York ou Genève.

КАК ПОЛУЧИТЬ ИЗДАНИЯ ОРГАНИЗАЦИИ ОБЪЕДИНЕННЫХ НАЦИЙ

Издания Организации Объединенных Наций можно купить в книжных магазинах
и агентствах во всех районах мира. Наводите справки об изданиях в вашем книжном
магазине или пишите по адресу: Организация Объединенных Наций, Секция по
продаже изданий, Нью-Йорк или Женева.

COMO CONSEGUIR PUBLICACIONES DE LAS NACIONES UNIDAS

Las publicaciones de las Naciones Unidas están en venta en librerías y casas distribuidoras en
todas partes del mundo. Consulte a su librero o diríjase a: Naciones Unidas, Sección de Ventas,
Nueva York o Ginebra.

Litho in United Nations, New York
14284—June 1998—2,700
ISBN 92-1-133603-1

United Nations publication
Sales No. E.98.V.11